T0067905

Tommy Boone and Ed Boone

WestBow Press books may be ordered through booksellers or by contacting:

WestBow Press
A Division of Thomas Nelson & Zondervan
1663 Liberty Drive
Bloomington, IN 47403
www.westbowpress.com
1 (866) 928-1240

ISBN: 978-1-9736-0136-4 (sc)

Print information available on the last page.

WestBow Press rev. date: 9/28/2017

Contents

Dedication

For Brenda, Barbara, and our children –
Toby, Tara, and Ed Jr. and Pamela

Acknowledgment

We want to thank our sister, Ginger Aaron. Without her editorial assistance and spiritual influence, this book would not have been possible. Also, we want to express our appreciation and sincere thanks to Nikki Mata, Check In Coordinator of WestBow Press, for her support and encouragement throughout the publishing process.

Foreword

> Do not be anxious about anything, but in everything, by prayer and petition, with thanksgiving, present your requests to God. And the peace of God, which transcends all understanding, will guard your hearts and your minds in Christ Jesus.
>
> – Philippians 4:6-7 BSB

IF THERE IS one thing that is known about **The Lord's Prayer**, it is this: It changes us. This is important when we are falling to pieces. For many people, life is not easy. There is conflict, loss of a job, and families disintegrate. Instead of finding a solution to problems, battle lines are formed. People get frustrated and angry. They look for their horse-shoe or rabbit's foot for power, but there is no good luck with either.

Life without prayer is a death trap. It is critical that every man and woman, regardless of age, find the time to pray The Lord's Prayer.

One critically important step in dealing with life's dilemmas and unpleasant experiences is to trust in Jesus Christ as the Son of God and say "yes" to prayer. This means trusting in God to help live in the present. It means pushing aside doubts and relying on **The Lord's Prayer** to affirm the good in life for Jesus said, "These things I have spoken unto you, that in me ye might have peace. In the world ye shall have tribulation: but be of good cheer; I have overcome the world" (John 16:33). Life is not hopeless.

> Faith has a powerful effect in helping people recover a sense of balance, tranquility, and hope. Indeed, I am persuaded that there is nothing in the arsenal of medical or psychological technology that equals the power inherent in a simple faith.
>
> – Robert L. Veninga

Preface

To pray is to make a mental and emotional connection to feel complete within the universe. It is the greatest gift from Jesus Christ and God to humanity. It doesn't matter who you are or the work you do, every person needs a personal relationship with our Spiritual Father in Heaven.

WRITING A BOOK can be a challenge, especially given there isn't enough time to invest in the search for ideas and organizing thoughts and feelings about a particular topic. But, it can also be a great experience. It can be exciting, and even a change in lifestyle. There are definitely moments when a writer stops to allow the mind to think of other things, if not to breathe, relax, and let ideas come to the surface. Writing is both fun and hard work much like exercise. The mental process of writing can be a great gift. As a new adventure, it is all about feelings and experiences. This is true for us as well.

The Christian resists evil with good, returns love for hate, and returns prayer for insult.

– David Abernathy

As brothers, we decided almost at the blink of an eye to write a book about **The Lord's Prayer**. Neither one of us was sure why we felt compelled to do so. But, after getting into the writing process, we realized it was something that each of us wanted to do. It was not written to call attention to either of us. It was written because we felt the need to better understand the "life changing power" of The

Lord's Prayer. This desire to do so came while we were on the Taylor Bayou in southeast Texas late one afternoon after a few hours of just riding, relaxing, and looking at God's gift of the bayou-world about us. It was a special afternoon in that it resulted in each of us thinking about God and His Son Jesus Christ.

Both of us have been around awhile. We have enjoyed our own direction in life and professional work of many years of different responsibilities. From early childhood throughout adulthood we remained close to Jesus Christ, particularly by way of our personal prayers. We are neither ordained ministers nor graduates of theology or religious studies. The canvas of our spiritual feelings is painted with evidence of prayer. We believe that Jesus died on the cross for our sins so that we might have life without end. Hence, it is our belief that God exists and that He is the Kingdom, Power, and Glory forever. This belief gives us hope of eternal life in Heaven. This is itself our credential of faith that guides and supports our passion to write on behalf of The Lord's Prayer and what it means to us.

God gives each of us a unique and personal purpose in life. Don't ever allow anyone to make you feel that prayer is useless and meaningless. We are meant to pray and testify the truth on behalf of Jesus Christ

This feeling we live with was instilled in us from an early age. Both our father and mother took us to the First Baptist Church in Leesville, Louisiana where we were baptized at 12 years of age. As you may know, baptism means to dip or immerse a person into water for religious reasons. In the opening gospel stories of the New Testament, John the Baptist baptized his disciples at Bethany beyond Jordan where Jesus met John and was baptized by him (John 1:25-34).

> ***What does it mean to not believe in John 3:16?*** *Consider these answers. Death and eternal life with Satan in hell on one hand and, and on the other, life and eternal happiness with God in Heaven.*

It is interesting how the mind can be trapped in a time warp of past events without the consideration and influence of new ideas later on. Such a condition of the mind can often keep people from experiencing meaning in life. In this instance though, our time spent in Church was not negative whatsoever. Our time spent in the First Baptist Church unlocked the gift of spiritual opportunity. That gift is Heaven where there are unseen and unknown God-provided realities waiting for us. Heaven is where Christians will spend eternity with God, Jesus Christ, and the Holy Spirit. There is no other place like it.

> We cannot be complacent about our need to pray, yet it is so common that we fail to pray (perhaps, partly due to the sense of being entertained by all the technology we have today).

Prayer provides inspiration for the depressed, and it motivates the discouraged. Without prayer, life would be a challenge and few would be able to make sense of living. With prayer, there is the courage to stay the course and see God's purpose completed in our lives on behalf of God, ourselves, and others. In particular, The Lord's Prayer motivates the believer in Christ to expand his or her influence on others and to help inspire and promote a new and transformative way of thinking and living on behalf of Jesus Christ, the Son of God, who died on the cross for our sins.

Our world today is in desperate need of personal and family

prayer. This point is highlighted by the fact that there are many who have no daily prayer moments in their lives. Moreover, they do not have any idea as to how to sit down and begin to pray. We believe reading this book chapter by chapter can help nurture, define, and capture prayer as a vital part of a person's life. We also hope to help the reader understand the intent of each petition in The Lord's Prayer. Reading the content more than once should encourage a difference in how a person sees and lives life. "The Lord's Prayer" is a powerful opportunity to speak to God, which is helpful in determining the reader's eternal destiny.

Next to John 3:16 and the 23rd Psalm, **The Lord's Prayer** is probably known by more people than any other passage of scripture. St. Thomas Aquinas (13th century AD) called it "the most perfect of all prayers". Tertullian (2nd century AD) called it the "summary of the whole gospel". Thus, our wish is that this book, **The Lord's Prayer**, will be the beginning for some to believe in John 3:16 and the strength for others who accept the prayer as central and fundamental to the values and priorities of our Christian faith.

> Delight thyself also in the Lord: and he shall give thee the desires of thine heart.
>
> – Psalm 37:4

Introduction

> People can be taught to *say* prayers, to *read* prayers, to *memorize* prayers, but they cannot be taught to *pray.* When the *relationship* exists, they pray instinctively. Anything else is mere words. That is what Jesus was teaching.
>
> – Everett L. Fullam and Bob Slosser

THE LORD'S PRAYER was given to us by Jesus Christ in the Sermon on the Mount. It is a prayer that addresses the Father of Heaven and Earth. When we pray, we are to speak it from our heart to demonstrate love for Jesus Christ who gave His life so that we might have eternal life with our Spiritual Father in Heaven. We do not need to preach a sermon to God when we pray. He already knows everything about us, what we need, and how often we fail to pray. Everyone who confesses Jesus Christ as savior is a member of God's family by trust and faith. They acknowledge that all power is God's and that God alone is worthy of glory today and in the future. Prayer and trust in God changes a person for the good.

Many people have been looking for God, but they don't pray. So, what do they end up with? Life is more than work and selfish needs.

Given the importance of prayer, how often do you pray The Lord's Prayer? No doubt it is one prayer that most Christians and many people throughout the world know by heart. It is also the prayer that Jesus Christ taught His disciples when they asked Him how to pray.

Do you think you will grow closer to God and His Son Jesus Christ if you were to pray it more frequently? We think so. To pray The Lord's Prayer is to know that we are in the presence of God in Heaven. It is a personal act of the heart in reverence, humility, and expectation to glorify and honor God according to His will and purpose.

To pray The Lord's Prayer with a childlike trust is a great blessing and gift from God who acknowledges us as His children. He understands our needs, our concerns, and our purpose in life. It is our faith in Jesus Christ, who gave us the perfect way to pray, that we come before God in confidence of being heard.

- ***Our Father*** is to whom we should pray to. He is our Heavenly Father and we are His children. Recall that Jesus told Mary Magdalene after His resurrection, "I ascend unto my Father, and your Father; and to my God, and your God" (John 20:17).
- ***Who Art in Heaven*** is a clear and powerful statement of the home of God and the place of eternal existence for all who believe in the Jesus Christ as the Son of God.
- ***Hallowed Be Thy Name*** is the first of seven petitions that states we are to worship God, to praise Him, and to acknowledge His holiness. He is pure and faultless. We can talk with, worship, and praise Him.
- When we pray the second petition, ***Thy Kingdom Come***, we are praying for God's rule on earth. It is also a reminder that we are to pray for God's Kingdom and purpose in our lives and not our own desires and wants.
- The third petition is ***Thy Will Be Done, on Earth as It Is in Heaven.*** It is a reminder to pray for God's will to be done, not our will. We are to align our will with God's will, and ask that His way triumphs.

- We are to ask God for the physical, mental, emotional, and spiritual needs in ***Give Us This Day Our Daily Bread.*** It is the fourth petition of which the purpose is to emphasize that we pray The Lord's Prayer so that we will not worry about tomorrow, for tomorrow will worry about itself. It is also a way of affirming that everything we are and have comes from God.
- ***Forgive Us Our Debts, as We Also Have Forgiven Our Debtors*** reminds us that we must confess our sins, shortcomings, and resentments to God and to turn from our sins and forgive others as God has forgiven us. This verse is known as the fifth petition.
- The sixth and seventh petitions, ***Lead Us Not into Temptation, but Deliver Us From Evil,*** are the final requests for protection by our Father in Heaven. Both petitions are a plea for help in achieving victory over sin and a request for protection from the attacks of Satan.
- ***For Thine Is the Kingdom and the Power and the Glory, Forever*** is praising God and recognizing life with Him and His eternal power.
- The word "***Amen***" means "so let it be". It gives us the opportunity to add our voice to the affirmations and petitions of **The Lord's Prayer**.

Why not take half an hour and read one page from each chapter followed by a brief reflection on the content? The primary thing about the content is that, while it is specific to each chapter heading, there is also an overlap of thoughts, feelings, and beliefs. This is considered necessary to get the full view of the content of God's involvement in our lives.

> **The Lord's Prayer** is the prayer Jesus Christ taught His disciples so that they would know how to pray.

The Lord's Prayer is both giving glory and praise to God "Our Father in Heaven" and the opportunity to ask forgiveness and help. We also learn that, while we are often slow in forgiving others, we know that we must forgive those who have trespassed against us just as God has forgiven us. For many people, forgiving what others have done to them at work, home, or elsewhere is believed to be impossible. But, the more you pray, worship, and confess your sins to God, you learn the importance of forgiving others. Also, you learn that when you pray to God, Our Father in Heaven, you are hopeful of receiving forgiveness of your sins. Even when it appears that your prayers are not being answered, you continue to pray anyway.

To pray The Lord's Prayer is to live a life in the will of God. It is our means to connecting with God. When we pray The Lord's Prayer, we are asking God to intervene in our lives. Remember, James 4:2, NIV says, "You do not have, because you do not ask God." We need to embrace the will of God so that all things will be possible in our lives. This is done through the authority of His Son, Jesus Christ, who gives us access to God's power and resources.

The LORD will fight for you; you need only to be still.

– Exodus 14:14 NIV

The Lord's Prayer is the perfect way to pray, and express our love for God if we are praying from our hearts and minds. But, to do so, we must avoid praying with empty words (such as when we are praying while thinking about something else). This is why Jesus cautioned the disciples before giving them the prayer. He said:

[5] And when you pray, do not be like the hypocrites, for they love to pray standing in the synagogues and on the street corners to be seen by others. Truly I tell you, they have received their reward in full. [6] But when you pray, go into your room, close the door and pray to your Father, who is unseen. Then your Father, who sees what is done in secret, will reward you. [7] And when you pray, do not keep on babbling like pagans, for they think they will be heard because of their many words. [8] Do not be like them, for your Father knows what you need before you ask him.

– Matthew 6:5-8 NIV

Chapter 1

Our Father

The Lord's Prayer is the best of all prayers. God's Son, Jesus Christ, taught us the prayer. It is the prayer to God "Our Father." We are "His" children and He is "Our" God.

THROUGHOUT THE SCRIPTURES, names are important. A person's name often stands for character or position. The word "father" is unique and special to most people. No doubt you have been asked the question, "Who is your father?" After you tell the person who he is, that person might say: "Oh, I know him. He was my high school teacher." Expressed in this way the word "father" identifies a person, career position, and relationship to you and others. But, in contrast to our human father, this chapter is about our Spiritual Father. The incredibly good news is that God has adopted us into His spiritual family through the sacrifice of His Son, Jesus Christ, on the cross.

In love he predestined us for adoption as sons through Jesus Christ, according to the purpose of his will.

– Ephesians 1:5 ESV

Before continuing the discussion of ***Our Father***, it is important to visit the opening line of The Lord's Prayer, as given by Jesus in the Sermon on the Mount. When Jesus prayed to God in Heaven, he used the words – Our Father. He told the disciples that His Father is

Our Father. Thus, when we pray, the sons and daughters of God are invited to come into the very presence of God the Father. The Lord's Prayer is a calling upon God in Heaven who rules over all things and all people. We can share with God the Father our needs and personal concerns. He cares about each of us, and we are blessed to call Our Father Who Art in Heaven our Spiritual Father (Matthew 6:9).

> We are "...all sons of God through faith in Christ Jesus" (Galatians 3:26 NKJV). Because you are sons, God sent the Spirit of his Son into our hearts, the Spirit who calls out, "Abba, Father". So you are no longer a slave, but a son; and since you are a son, God has made you also an heir (Galatians 4:6-7 NKJV).

God Hears Our Prayers

To know that God is always listening to our prayers is a powerful feeling of comfort when we are happy or sad with feelings of being hurt or depressed. Our instinct is to connect with someone to feel alive and safe. When we pray, we connect with ***Our Father*** in Heaven. The words "Our Father" are a powerful mental and emotional refuge where we restore our will to live and gain strength to begin again.

Just as Jesus Christ prayed frequently to Our Heavenly Father, we must draw close to God by addressing him as Our Father. The idea of God's fatherhood is huge, especially when we are weak in spirit without the spiritual passion we need to live. It is also true when we are stripped of laughter and happiness. The fact is this: Our Father who art in heaven is our sanctuary. We are part of God's family.

As pointed out in John 3:16, "For God so loved the world, that he gave his only begotten Son, that whosoever believeth in him should not perish, but have everlasting life." God loves us. Our Father in

Heaven hears our prayers. We have no reason to be anxious about anything. Instead, we can be confident that "...whoever believes in him shall not perish but have eternal life." We are heirs of God and co-heirs with Jesus Christ the Son of God. In fact, note what Romans 8:14-17 ESV says,

> [14] For all who are led by the Spirit of God are sons of God. [15] For you did not receive the spirit of slavery to fall back into fear, but you have received the Spirit of adoption as sons, by whom we cry, "Abba! Father!" [16] The Spirit himself bears witness with our spirit that we are children of God, [17] and if children, then heirs —heirs of God and fellow heirs with Christ, provided we suffer with him in order that we may also be glorified with him.

We are children of God ***Our Father*** in Heaven. As members of God's family, we pray that God's name will be recognized as Holy. This first petition of The Lord's Prayer is closely akin to the Third Commandment of the Ten Commandments, "Thou shall not take the name of the Lord thy God in vain." Thus, we all share the same responsibility to bring honor and glory to God's name in the way we talk about God and the way in which we worship God. To "Hallow God's Name" is to put him at the center of our worship whether we are at home, work, or church. To do so is to remind us that God is holy and exalted, set apart from sin.

...to all who received Him, who believed in His name, He gave power to become children of God; who were born, not of blood nor of the will of the flesh nor of the will of man, but of God.

– John 1:12 ESV

To pray is to open one's heart and soul in belief that "...ye receive them, and ye shall have them" (Mark 11:24). It is the desire of those who love Him and live to do His will that they keep God's name holy and sacred and seek His Kingdom. They believe that God loves and cares for them, and that belief makes living in a world of danger, risk, evil, and death worth the effort. Thus, the relationship of God as the creator of the universe and all things part of it and they who believe in God live a unique existence with the request "Lord, teach us to pray". It is Jesus who gives the world the prayer of hope. Even though our behaviors are often contrary to God our Father, as was the case with Adam and Eve, we are still connected to God's love. We pray to speak with God, to express our love, joy, and sorrow, and to confess our sins.

To say ***Our Father*** is to desire the spiritual relationship with God in Heaven. The Lord's Prayer is a powerful beginning point to realize the majestic existence to which we aspire in Heaven with God. But, given its focus on God, it should also be pointed out that The Lord's Prayer was meant to be a model or a pattern of prayer to Our Father and not as a substitute for praying our own prayers. Of course, it is important to remember why we pray. Prayer is acknowledging God's sovereignty and righteousness. We pray for God's help to conform to His desires in our lives. It is not about trying to get God to agree with our desires.

When we pray in reverence and respect for God's greatness and holiness. We pray to Our Father for His forgiveness. We pray so we can create Heaven on earth, knowing that He "...loved the world that He gave His only begotten Son that whosoever believeth in Him should not perish but have everlasting life" (John 3:16).

Teach Us How to Pray

The purpose of The Lord's Prayer is to teach us how to pray. Jesus Christ gave the prayer to the disciples as a guide for them. He told the disciples to pray to Our Father in Heaven, and to do so in a room with the door shut. The point that Jesus was making is that prayer should be a private matter between God the Father and those who believe in Him. A meaningless repetition of words or prayers is not the point of The Lord's Prayer or praying other prayers to God. What is important is the quality of the prayer and not its quantity.

The following questions should be considered by every Christian when asked, "How do you pray?" Is praying to ***Our Father Who Art in Heaven*** a priority? If not, why is that the case? If you make prayer a priority in your life, is there a time and place as a regular spiritual practice? If it is interrupted, how do you resume praying? Are you honest and humble? Are you personal? Is your prayer from the heart? Or, is it more intellectual in text and presentation? Do you pray the same prayer each day or a different prayer? How do you avoid praying "like the hypocrites" Jesus talked about in Matthew 6:5-6? Do you understand The Lord's Prayer is a great privilege and gift to us? Do you feel that your prayers are influenced and guided by the Holy Spirit?

When someone asked a nineteenth-century spiritual teacher about cultivating a deeper prayer life, she replied, "Say the Lord's Prayer, but take an hour to say it."

– Timothy Jones, The Art Of Prayer

After reviewing the questions just identified and time to reflect on your personal thoughts, it should be evident that the reasons for prayer and why Christians pray vary from one person to the next. What is important to understand is that The Lord's Prayer is a model for praying. The focus of the prayer is communication with God. What we say to God in prayer is in response to our challenges, given that we are struggling against the forces of evil. Also, it is asking questions such as "Lord, what do you want me to do?" What is God instructing Christians to think and feel are over-arching principles of addressing

God as Our Father in Heaven, which raises a very important question: "How did God become our Father?" The answer is found in the following scriptures.

> [26] So in Christ Jesus you are all children of God through faith, [27] for all of you who were baptized into Christ have clothed yourselves with Christ. [28] There is neither Jew nor Gentile, neither slave nor free, nor is there male and female, for you are all one in Christ Jesus. [29] If you belong to Christ, then you are Abraham's seed, and heirs according to the promise.
>
> – Galatians 3:26-29 NIV

Reconciled to God

Our relationship in prayer with God our Father in Heaven is through the intercession of His Son, Jesus Christ, and what He has done and where He now is, seated at the Father's right hand, and the indwelling Holy Spirit that makes intercessions for us. The death, burial, and resurrection of Jesus made it possible to be reconciled to God the Father of Heaven and eternity. Jesus made it possible to ask God "Our Father" for His mercy during challenging times to guide our actions and thoughts.

> [3] For what I received I passed on to you as of first importance: that Christ died for our sins according to the Scriptures, [4] that he was buried, that he was raised on the third day according to the Scriptures, [5] and that he appeared to Cephas, and then to the Twelve. [6] After that, he appeared to more than five hundred of the brothers and sisters at the same time, most of whom are still living, though some have fallen asleep.
>
> – 1 Corinthians 15:3-6 NIV

God, our Father in Heaven, sent His only Son, Jesus Christ, to satisfy that judgment for those who believe in Him. After living a sinless life, Jesus died for our sins on the cross. He was buried and on the third day rose from the dead. If we believe and trust this in our heart, and if we receive Jesus as our Savior, declaring, "Jesus is Lord," we will be saved to spend eternity with God, ***Our Father*** in Heaven. It is critical that we look to God, to seek to know Him, to depend on Him, and to share our thoughts and dreams with Him, our family and friends, and to thank Him for the gift of His love and hope.

> Let Us Pray,
> Eternal God, our loving and compassionate Father, we ask you to enter our hearts and minds and take away any obstacles to prayer. Help us to feel as comfortable in our communication with you as we do with a trusted friend.
> Amen
>
> – Bob Hansel

Ask in Prayer

The power of prayer should be self-evident, but that is not always the case. More often than not, we ask ourselves many times, "Why is it that we make poor choices in life?" "Why can't I get my life together and do what is right?" According to R. A. Torrey, the answer to these questions is that we neglect to pray and, therefore, we fail to receive God's blessings. This point was made clear in James 4:2, "Ye have not, because ye ask not."

The Holy Spirit is promised to every believer that he may obtain the supernatural gifts that qualify him for a particular service to which God calls him.

– R. A. Torrey
The Power of Prayer

Praying to ***Our Father*** in Heaven is God's gift to us. But, to manifest miracles we must ask in prayer, and we must do so continually in prayer. This point is critical. As pointed out in Psalm 19:14, "the words of my mouth, and the meditation of my heart, be acceptable in thy sight...." Also, we learn by faith in prayer that we are kept from temptation and delivered from the power of the wicked one. It is a deterrent to sin in our lives, thus prayer changes us.

> [14] This is the confidence we have in approaching God: that if we ask anything according to his will, he hears us. [15] And if we know that he hears us – whatever we ask – we know that we have what we asked of him.
>
> – I John 5:14-15 NIV

As St. Thomas Aquinas taught, "The Lord's prayer is the most perfect of prayers ... In it we not only ask for all the things we can rightly desire, but also in the sequence that we ought to desire them. Thus this prayer not only teaches us to ask for things, but also in what order we ought to desire them." For example, the first three petitions are more like blessings that acknowledge holiness of his name, his reign, and the acceptance of God's authority throughout all creation. Petitions four through seven make specific reference to our needs as children of ***Our Father*** in Heaven.

Just as it was taught to the disciples, Jesus invites us to pray The Lord's Prayer for God's presence and power to change us from the path of Hell to Heaven. So, do not rush through the words without understanding what they mean. Remember always, Jesus said "I am the way and the truth and the life. No one comes to the Father except through me" (John 14:6 NIV). Thus, it is critical that we pray to God as "Our Father" who is also "in Heaven".

So, to that end, set aside a time and a place for prayer. Pray at a personal level to ***Our Father.*** Be specific and honest about life's struggles and fears. Use ***The Lord's Prayer*** as a starting point. It will help you to keep in touch with Our Father in Heaven. Remember, it is a privilege to pray to ***Our Father in Heaven***. So ask for things that are in harmony with God's Will for: "This is the confidence that we have in Him, that if we ask anything according to His Will, He hears us" (1 John 6:14 NIV).

Chapter 2

Who Art in Heaven

We address God as "Our Father who art in Heaven" because we belong to Him. Why? We are His children the moment we accept Jesus Christ as His Son, our Savior who died on the cross for our sins.

WHERE IS HEAVEN? What does ***Who Art in Heaven*** mean? Well son, it is complicated, then, he took a deep breath, paused, and realized that he did not have an answer. So, he repeated the question several times to himself while walking a few steps away from his son hoping that something would click. The short of it is that he did not know beyond the simplest interpretation, which seemed too basic to be correct. Being a smart man and a good father, he told his son that he would take some time to think about it.

Where is Heaven? What is Heaven like? The more he thought about it the more questions he had. The bottom line is that talking about the Earth is challenging enough. To talk about Heaven is not an easy task. While we understand that God created Adam and Eve to live on the Earth, why did God pick Earth to be the place where humans would live? How is Earth different from the other planets? Is it likely

Each one of us who is baptized and who believes in Jesus Christ as the Son of God, and who seeks forgiveness for sin will find that Heaven's doors are open for them.

– John 3:3-5 NIV

there are other life forms like us or even different from us elsewhere in the Universe? If that is the case, are they confused about Heaven and what it is? Where are they? Will we talk to them? Are they on the other side of Heaven and, if so, where?

The son's questions got his father to thinking. The more the father worked at it the more difficult and challenging it became for him. Fortunately, the Christian faith is based on the notion that God is real. Our faith in God is the key connection to knowing eternal life and accepting that Heaven is the place where God the Creator of Earth exists. Imagine a universe so large that no one is in position to know it much less to explain where it is or to offer a rational explanation of it. Yet, most of us find ourselves believing that it exists. Why? The short answer is that we believe it is the right thing to do. Many of us do so because we were taught early on that God is real and that His Son, Jesus Christ, is real.

Today, we ask the question, did God create everything there is everywhere? According to the Bible, He must have, right? Once again, why did God attach himself to Earth? Was Earth God's first thought? Did God create the Earth? When did God know that He intended to visit Earth in the person of His Son, Jesus Christ? Were there other people living on Earth like us before Adam and Eve? If so, where were they when the great universe of planets and galaxies were formed? Did the Earth as we know it today exist before Adam and Eve or elsewhere in an entirely different form? As these questions and more passed through the father's mind, it became apparent that he did not know the answers to his son's questions.

Where Is Heaven?

Are our feelings about Heaven the same for everybody, male and female regardless of age? Is Heaven a "one-Heaven" for those who believe in Jesus Christ as the Son of God? Or, given that God is omnipotent and omnipresent, is there more than one Heaven or a timeline for multiple Heavens for different agendas? Is there an intermediate Heaven, that is, a temporary Heaven when we die? Is there an eternal Heaven where we will live with God?

As finite creatures we are not just poorly prepared on many fronts, we are seriously flawed and diminished by sin. Without God and Jesus Christ we are lost. Forgiveness is not automatic with death. There is no Heaven without repenting of our sins. Fortunately, the gift of Jesus Christ moves us from false doctrine and the struggles of life to live in faith that the gift of God is eternal life. " For it is by grace you have been saved, through faith — and this is not from yourselves, it is the gift of God — not by works, so that no one can boast" (Ephesians 2:8-9 NIV).

It is believed that God has no limitations. It is believed that there is only one God, one eternal Heaven, and one Son that we acknowledge having said, "not my will, by thy will be done." God is the ultimate expression of the Universe of which He created. He is almighty and eternal. Thus, we must confess our sins and God will forgive us of sins and purify us from all unrighteousness (1 John 1:9).

To live in Heaven is to be saved from Satan and hell.

To live in Heaven is to be with and loved by Our Spiritual Father.

Our Father ***Who Art in Heaven*** bonds us to our faith in prayer that God is "there" – wherever Heaven is – so is God. This part of The Lord's Prayer informs us that when we pray to God in Heaven we are praying in faith that God and Heaven coexist. Prayer is the means to thinking beyond the boundaries of the Earth. It is our personal connection to God in Heaven, on Earth, and throughout the Universe. It is God who supports our prayers, promotes our personal relationship with Him, and gives us the power and the determination to move beyond our mistakes and limitations. He loves us, comforts us, and nourishes us. It is therefore critically important that we pray to God as ***Our Father Who Art in Heaven*** who wants us to share our needs and concerns in prayer.

Heaven is where all the unknowns and fears are put aside. There are no more mistakes. As they say, life is good. It is absolute purity; an existence that is not possible on the present Earth or even on a different planet. It is a place of reverence. It is a place of existence with God, His Angels, and the Saints, and all others who believed in His Son, Jesus Christ. By faith, every Christian on the face of the Earth believes that Heaven is a destination for our soul after death.

All of this is true because in John 8:23 NIV, Jesus said, "You are from below; I am from above. You are of this world; I am not of this world." Jesus is from Heaven. After the crucifixion and the resurrection of Jesus, He returned to His Father, God, in Heaven, which goes beyond space, time, and distance.

In Revelation 21:11 NIV, Heaven is described in this way, "It shone with the glory of God, and its brilliance was like that of a very precious jewel, like a jasper, clear as crystal." This is certainly not a description of Earth for it is defined by sin and mortality. In Heaven, God's dwelling place, there is eternity and immortality with our Heavenly Father and, according to the apostle Paul (2 Corinthians 12:2), there are different 'levels' of Heaven (who describes his journey to the Third Heaven). Well, if that doesn't get your attention, nothing is likely to do so. Whether this verse refers to interstellar space (i.e., paradise) is unclear.

It is likely that the biggest difficulty the father had in answering his son's question, "What is Heaven?" is that no one knows what Heaven looks like. It is not a temple or a mountain. That is why the idea of Heaven being "up there" is beyond our earthly ability to comprehend. Point in fact, as St. Paul said when speaking to the Corinthians, "But as it is written, Eye hath not seen, nor ear heard, neither have entered into the heart of man, the things which God hath prepared for them that love him" (1 Corinthians 2:9).

Heaven is the community of all believers of Jesus Christ.

Imagine seeing God's face in Heaven. Imagine coming face to face (1 Corinthians 13:12; 1 John 3:2) with the creator of the world, the ultimate decision maker in what is good and bad, the Father of Jesus Christ, the creator of Adam and Eve, and the power of eternal life. Everyone who dies in God's grace will experience the rewards of Heaven, including the company of the angels. Heaven is the ultimate fulfillment of life and happiness. The Bible tells us that Heaven is God's house where, according to Revelations 21:4, "There will be no more tears, no more pain, and no more sorrow."

The word "Heaven" is used 238 times in the New Testament. The Old Testament refers to the "First" Heaven as sky where birds fly above us. The "Second" Heaven is recognized as the interstellar or outer space (i.e., the stars, planets, and other celestial objects) (Genesis 1:14-18). The dwelling place of God is the "Third" Heaven. Its location is not identified. The apostle John witnessed that Heaven (the New Earth) possesses the glory of God (Revelation 21:11) where there is no night and God is the light, the sun, and the moon (Revelation 22:5). The city John describes is filled with costly stones and crystal clear jasper with twelve gates (Revelation 21:12) and the wall of the city had twelve foundations (Revelation 21:14). The paradise of the Garden of Eden is restored. As Revelation 22:1-2 BSB says, "The river of the water of life, as clear as crystal, flowing from the throne of God and of the Lamb down the middle of the great street of the city. On each side of the river stood the tree of life, bearing twelve crops of fruit, yielding its fruit every month. And the leaves of the tree are for the healing of the nations."

Heaven Is a Real Place

Only those who believe in Jesus Christ as the Son of God and die in God's grace will be saved. Only they will enter Heaven and live with God forever. Heaven is a real place. God's throne is Heaven (Isaiah 66:1), which is beyond all limitations of this universe as we know it. It is where Jesus was taken up into Heaven to sit at the right hand of God (Mark 16:19). It is Jesus who promised an eternal home in Heaven. Hence, we are able to endure life's challenges, disappointments, and hardships. Heaven is without pain or sadness because the Father of our Lord Jesus Christ has reconciled Heaven and Earth. This way of being is a commandment from God to love one another as He loves us, thus defining the significance of The Lord's Prayer.

> Strong Son of God, Immortal Love, Whom we, that have not seen thy face, by faith, and faith alone embrace.
>
> – Alfred, Lord Tennyson (1809-1892)

When we share with others The Lord's Prayer and, then say **Who Art in Heaven** - children are likely to think of God somewhere "out there" in space and time. God's immediate presence is transient even though there might be some sense of His personal relationship in all things and places. It is this mental and emotional feeling that we are talking to God that is for now our reality of Heaven. Its place is where we are at the moment, and it is wherever God is. Our mindset and prayer opens up Heaven to us where we are without knowledge of its location. Otherwise, for those who do not love God,

Our Father who art in Heaven.

– Matthew 6:9

they will not know Heaven until they believe in Jesus Christ as the Son of God.

As noted in Genesis 1:1 NIV, "In the beginning God created the Heavens and the Earth." While we have learned what Earth is, nothing about living on Earth explains Heaven. Regardless of our experiences, what we have come to believe, and how we might want to describe Heaven, it is beyond our capacity to do so. Yet, God is the essence of Heaven. Thinking about God now while we are on Earth may be Heaven. Living the Christian lifestyle and believing in God while we are on Earth may be Heaven just as much as dying today is thought necessary to go to Heaven. Maybe Heaven is a place where there is no boundary defined by time or space. Maybe our faith is in fact the ultimate frontier of time and space with God and His Son. After all, God's spirit fills all space and time. There is no reason to worry about the destination of Heaven because God said there is a Heaven waiting for us (John 14:2).

> Surely it is not wrong for us to think and talk about Heaven. I like to find out all I can about it. I expect to live there through all eternity. If I were going to dwell in any place in this country, if I were going to make it my home, I would inquire about its climate, about the neighbors I would have — about everything, in fact, that I could learn concerning it. If soon you were going to emigrate, that is the way you would feel. Well, we are all going to emigrate in a very little while. We are going to spend eternity in another world … Is it not natural that we should look and listen and try to find out who is already there and what is the route to take?
>
> – D. L. Moody

Eternity in Heaven

While living forever is an interesting thought, spending eternity in Heaven is a fantastic thought. The ticket to Heaven is Jesus Christ. Remember this: When we ask Jesus Christ for forgiveness and a new way to live in order to keep God's commandments, He will freely give us both. Jesus died on the cross for our sins. When we ask for forgiveness, it opens the door of God's dwelling place where there are mansions and vineyards for those who are faithful to His Word. In fact, Jesus told his disciples, "...I will not drink of this fruit of the vine from now on until that day when I drink it new with you in My Father's Kingdom" (Matthew 26:29 NKJV).

> **Jesus Christ** said, "I am the way, the truth, and the life. No one comes to the Father except through Me."
>
> – John 14:6 NIV

Failing to ask Jesus for forgiveness separates us from God. However common, this is one of the most important and most neglected aspects of Christian study. Yet, that is why the breaking of God's Law will keep us from entering Heaven. This speaks to every person on Earth, given that every single person is a sinner and has come short of the glory of God (Romans 3:23). Hence, the gift of eternal life in Heaven begins with confessing our sins so that we can be cleansed from all unrighteousness (1 John 1:9). Only then, this paradise of eternity, that is, the Kingdom where both Heaven and Earth unite is experienced as unimaginable spiritual and physical dimensions that transcend time and space. It is a place where there will be no sin or suffering. It is where there will be no pain and sorrow. Both will be replaced with happiness, comfort, peace, joy, and knowledge.

Hence, Heaven is the opposite of eternal punishment in Hell. As

Revelation 21:4 NKJV says, "...God will wipe away every tear from their eyes; there shall be no more death, nor sorrow, nor crying. There shall be no more pain, for the former things have passed away." Heaven is God's home. It is the dwelling place of Christians. Where God is, Heaven is as well. His dwelling place is the limitless immensity of God, glory, and immortality. It is a state of being, here and now, not in some distant space far away.

[21] nor will they say, 'See here!' or 'See there!' For indeed, the kingdom of God is within you.

– Luke 17:21 NKJV

Isn't it a wonderful thing that our Heavenly Father sent His Son to be our Savior and show us the way to live according to His plan? We are the adopted children God has chosen to be with Him in Heaven. Our responsibility is to believe in Jesus Christ, to follow His teachings, and to repent when we commit sins. By faith, we can do our part to help ensure that our lives will not end when we die. We must face life with its problems to find rest with God. In agreement, the words of St. Augustine indicate that, "You created us for you, O Lord, and our hearts are restless until they find their rest in you."

> ***God Is Our Father.*** While we live, grow old, and die on Earth, we live forever in Heaven. We have a divine destiny. After all, God created us, looks over us, and is with us throughout eternity.

Glorifying God

With this thought in mind, our responsibility in doing our part is to pray The Lord's Prayer. The beauty of this point is that The Lord's Prayer is designed to give us access to God. ***Our Father Who Art in***

Heaven is not just a combination of words. When we pray it, we are gathered in His name. It does not matter where we are or what we are faced with, God hears our prayers. God is everywhere, day or night, at work or play, while we are jogging or fixing something in the house. God helps us as we face life and its ups and downs. God is "the" one and the "only one" who is not created.

You are worthy, O Lord and God, to receive glory and honor and power, for You created all things, and by Your will they exist and were created.

– Revelation 4:11 BSB

Our Father Who Art in Heaven hears our prayers when we are strong or afraid, when we are laughing or crying, and when we are driving our car or painting the house. We can pray The Lord's Prayer and know that God hears us and is with us. We are connected, and our relationship is for eternity. The cross made this prayer possible. Jesus said, "I ascend unto my Father, and your Father; and to my God, and your God" (John 20:17).

> Father, Lord of Heaven and Earth, I ask in Your name, God the Father, for Your mercy. For I rejoice in You, knowing my sins are forgiven. Thank you for the gift of prayer.

All of life glorifies God, especially when we live to fulfill the purpose that God has given to each of us. This is as God desires; a plan not made by man, but by His own hand to give us victory, happiness, and joy. That is why it is important to think positive and put aside the disappointments of our friends, family members, and colleagues. No matter how we may experience the day, no matter how the month has gone by, no matter how we may wish the circumstances had been different, life is too valuable not to forgive and glorify God.

To glorify God is to acknowledge Him in honor of creating all things. To love God is to glorify Him. To ask for forgiveness of our sins is to glorify God. When we believe in John 3:16, we glorify God by believing in Jesus Christ as His Son who died on the cross for our sins. We glorify God by praying The Lord's Prayer, and we glorify God by living the Christian life, praising God, and giving glory to God for all that we are and do.

...Let your light so shine before men, that they may see your good works and glorify your Father in heaven.

– Matthew 5:16 BSB

Knowing that we are a creation of God helps us to see daily work as a blessing and a gift without pressure to out-perform others. This understanding comes from the ever-present knowledge that Jesus Christ did everything necessary to restore our relationship with Him. So why not work and live in joy and the expectation of eternal life with Him in Heaven?

> God is a God of glory. God is glorious. God exists to be glorified. The Bible speaks of the glory of God as a mega-theme that appears about 275 times in the English translation, 50 times alone in the book of Psalms.
>
> – Mark Driscoll

We were made to glorify God. Paul said in 1 Corinthians 10:31 NIV, "Whether you eat or drink or whatever you do, do it all to the glory of God." Hence, it is clear that we should glorify God every moment of every day. This means at home, with friends, while working, and all other places and opportunities. We glorify our Heavenly Father when we share His name with our family, friends, colleagues, and the world, when we cast all our concerns upon Him, and when we fret for nothing. After all, God loves us, cares for us, and has given His Son, Jesus Christ, who gave His life for us. We are blessed for the Bible is full of truth and love. There is no need to worry for Jesus Christ has delivered us from evil.

> ***Listen to the Psalmist, Psalm 29:1-2***. Give unto the Lord, O ye mighty; give unto the Lord glory. Give unto the Lord the glory due unto His name; worship the Lord in the beauty of holiness.

Most certainly, we learn to glorify God ***Who Art in Heaven*** whether we are eating or working in the yard (1 Corinthians 10:31). We glorify God when we praise Him, when we believe in His Son, when we trust Him with our lives, when we serve God with gladness, when we promote our salvation, when we turn others away from Satan to God, when we pray to Our Father, when we ask for the forgiveness of sins, and when we go about doing good. It is also a privilege to glorify God when we come into His presence with singing (Psalm 100:2).

Do Not Worry

Our Father in Heaven is God in our own consciousness. It is not a geographical location. God transcends anything we can think of or describe. Yet, He is ever-present. He hears our prayers, and it is through our prayers that we face life with its good and bad moments. Whether Heaven is referred to as the Kingdom of Heaven or the Kingdom of God does not matter. God is everywhere, even within us. Hence, we need to cultivate the spiritual possibilities within our

[15] Then the seventh angel blew his trumpet, and there were loud voices in heaven, saying, "The kingdom of the world has become the kingdom of our Lord and of his Christ, and he shall reign forever and ever."

– Revelation 11:15 ESV

hearts and minds. Remember, Jesus said that "The Kingdom of God is within you" (Luke 17:21).

Common sense tells us that if everyone lived with God within them, prayer would be more abundant and problems would disappear. But, our personal reality based on our free will, which is given to us by Our Father, is selfish and sinful. When we really understand this thinking, we can honestly say we need faith, prayer, and God's guidance. We need personal contact with the Creator of the universe, God. For those who believe in God, He is not just the Creator of the universe, He is also the life-giving Spirit who lives in us. He is our Redeemer and Savior who is near to us and is available to us anytime and anywhere to meet our needs.

St. Augustine said, "You created us for you, O Lord, and our hearts are restless until they find their rest in you." God's will for us is to know Him and to experience joy and love while on the Earth as in Heaven. We know God through prayer, and we grow stronger trusting in Him to meet our needs (i.e., "daily bread"). By supplying us our daily needs, we focus on His purpose for us while on Earth.

Note what Matthew 6:25-34 NIV, said about God's guarantee to be our provider. [25] Therefore I tell you, do not worry about your life, what you will eat or drink; or about your body, what you will wear. Is not life more than food, and the body more than clothes? [26] Look at the birds of the air; they do not sow or reap or store away in barns, and yet your heavenly Father feeds them. Are you not much more valuable than they? [27] Can any one of you by worrying add a single hour to your life? [28] And why do you worry about clothes? See how the flowers of the field grow. They do not labor or spin. [29] Yet I tell you that not even Solomon in all his splendor was dressed like one of these. [30] If that is how God clothes the grass of the field, which is here today and tomorrow is thrown into the fire, will he not much more clothe you – you of little faith? [31] So do not worry, saying, 'What shall we eat?' or 'What shall we drink?' or 'What shall we wear?' [32] For the pagans run after all these things, and your heavenly Father knows that you need them. [33] But seek first his kingdom and his righteousness, and all these things will be given to you as well. [34] Therefore do not worry about tomorrow, for tomorrow will worry about itself. Each day has enough trouble of its own.

> ***Key Point:*** Seek God's Kingdom and do not worry about things beyond your influence. After all, your home is not Earth. If you are one with God, then, your home is Heaven. Do not worry!

Chapter 3

Hallowed Be Thy Name

Sacred is God's name, as so completely understood by angels from Heaven, that every Christian father who ask to receive God's blessings for his family glorifies God's name.

JESUS SAID, BEGIN praying by glorifying the name of God – ***Hallowed Be Thy Name***. Why, because He is God. We are to praise and show reverence to His name. Moreover, we are commanded not to use God's name in thoughtless ways. The word "hallow" means "to recognize as holy" or "to treat in a holy way". Thus, by not using the name of God in a careless way, we honor God by showing respect for His name. This is done when we pray and worship Him. It is done when we acknowledge that God is in control of all things of this world and beyond, and that God has authority over all that is and will be.

Effective prayer doesn't require a Ph.D. – it only requires a willingness to share your thoughts with God.

– Joni Eareckson Tada

Praising God, our savior, is good for us and all the living things of the world. We praise Him for His name. We praise Him for His greatness. We glorify God the Father, Jesus the Son, and the Holy Spirit because they are worthy of our praise. The more we obey God the more joy we bring to Him and ourselves. Isn't that a glorious thought? Thus, when we pray to God, Lord of the universe, we travel through the mystery of time to find ourselves at His feet. We praise God and bring joy to His Kingdom when we ask God to help us persevere, to strengthen us, and to intercede on our behalf and that of our family and friends. This is why we must never neglect praying and pouring out our spirit to God, Almighty.

> Do not be afraid – I am with you! I am your God – let nothing terrify you! I will make you strong and help you; I will protect you and save you.
>
> – Isaiah 41:10 GNT

The more we praise God, the more we move closer to understanding our need to pray and to seek His help in all things we do. The more we pray to God, the more we are purged of sin. Our faith in God guides us to be disciplined in prayer and in being good children of God. His holy presence in our lives helps us to understand that sin is incompatible with God's Holiness.

When we trust God with everything that is vital to us, we find ourselves giving praise to God and sharing His love for us. John 3:16 highlights this point: ***"For God so loved the world, that he gave his only begotten Son, that whosoever believeth in him shall not perish but have everlasting life."*** This is "the" verse in the Bible that speaks to the heart of Christianity. It is the key to understanding that everlasting life begins and ends with God, "the Alpha and Omega, the First and Last, the Beginning and End" (Revelation 22:13 NIV). Giving praise to God in prayer is to honor God for His love and wisdom that provides meaning in life.

Reborn in the Spirit of God

To be reborn in the Spirit of God, it is necessary that we believe in Jesus Christ as the Divine One who we yearn to know and to listen to our prayers. After all, the only path to Heaven is as John 3:18 says, "He that believeth in Him is not condemned: but he that believeth not is condemned already, because he hath not believed in the name of the only begotten Son of God."

It is the responsibility of those who seek God to pray abundantly, as so clearly stated by Charles H. Spurgeon: "The more we pray, the more we shall want to pray. The more we pray, the more we can pray. The more we pray, the more we shall pray. He who prays little will pray less, but he who prays much will pray more, and he who prays more will desire to pray more abundantly."

We will be judged by what we have not done, by the love we have not shown.

– Henry Drummond

In prayer we open ourselves to a relationship with God that changes us by creating a personal reality, which aligns our thinking in accordance with a Christian communion with God. The meaning of "holiness" is an integral part of the grace of God. It helps us to come to an understanding of who we are and how to love ourselves. The implications are huge because God is within each of us, helping us to know who we are and why we find ourselves doing what we do. While this level of thinking is not without earthly challenges, the best we can do is to have the courage to stay the course through faith in Jesus Christ.

> ***To enter the Kingdom of God***, we need the conviction to pray, speak, and live with passion to give, build, and create the right way to think about God.
>
> Dear Heavenly Father,
> Today, I know that my sins are forgiven. I pray that I will always keep my thoughts on You and that You will engage me in work for Your glory. Teach me to be kind and helpful to others. Help me to stay grounded in faith and conviction, and committed to a lifetime of prayer. Give me a clear mind to make the right decisions. Help me Lord to understand what you have shaped me to do. I ask these things in Your Son's name, Jesus Christ.
> Amen.

The reality of this thinking helps to create a personal relationship with Jesus Christ who was sent by His Father in Heaven to die on the cross to pay the price for our sins. Because God knows that we become what we think about, what we talk about, and what we do, we ask in prayer for Christ to come into our hearts for salvation and deliverance.

> "Very truly I tell you, whoever hears my word and believes him who sent me has eternal life and will not be judged but has crossed over from death to life."
>
> – John 5:24 NIV

As an example of this thinking, the following prayer is an excellent beginning point when speaking to Our Father in Heaven. It was written by Virginia (Ginger) Aaron.

Help Me God

Dear Heavenly Father, I need your help.
Help me for I hit bottom.
And I am afraid of my thoughts.

Help me grow beyond my arrogance to be a better person.
Please cleanse me of my sins.
Come into my life.

I believe in Jesus Christ, your Son.
I believe Jesus Christ died for my sins.
I believe in the Holy Spirit.
I believe He will judge the living and the dead.
I believe in forgiveness of sins and everlasting
life with you in Heaven.

Dear God, I know that I am a sinner.
I need your forgiveness.
I need you in my life.
Help me to live in ways of righteousness and truth.
Open my heart and be with me.
In Your Son's Name, Jesus Christ.
Amen.

With God's presence there is light, help, peace, and refuge. We can understand the world better with God directing our lives. There is a peace deep within each of us knowing that God helps us to think the right thoughts. Marcus Aurelius, known as the wisest man of ancient Rome said it this way, "Our life is what our thoughts make of it." Hence, "If we confess our sins, he is faithful and just to forgive us our sins, and to cleanse us from all unrighteousness" (1 John 1:9). We are forgiven of our sins and at peace with God, given that the Holy Spirit within each of us will teach us all things we need to know so that we may have the assurance of eternal life after death.

Give Glory to God

When we pray ***Hallowed Be Thy Name***, it is God we honor. We are giving glory to ***Our Father in Heaven*** who loves us and gave us His Son for our salvation. St. Gregory of Nyssa, a Church Father in Cappadocia in Asia Minor, wrote around 380 AD that "of all good things the most important for me is that God's name should be glorified in my life." Armed with God's Spirit and the truth of His Name and Word, we are prepared to deal with our trials and temptations created by Satan.

The sanctification of God's name is the *first petition* in The Lord's Prayer. This first of seven requests is to make sure that God's Name is regarded as Holy, which means that we are to pray in His presence with reverence and respect. As children of God, we are drawn to His presence with feelings of joy and happiness for He is worthy of our love and worship. We pray even when we are not good at it. We do so because God is the reason we pray. We do not pray to impress others.

Perhaps the best way to understand the role of the Trinity in prayer is that we pray to the Father, through (or in the name of) the Son, by the power of the Holy Spirit. All three are active participants in the believer's prayer.

– www.gotquestions.org/pray-Father-Son-Spirit.html

We worship God and only God, and often we pray to our triune God (Father, Son, and Holy Spirit) because we are honoring His name and the coming of His kingdom. To pray to one member of the Trinity is prayer to all three because they are one!

> ***To Pray is to Give Glory to God.*** "I am the LORD: that is my name! I will not yield my glory to another or my praise to idols."
>
> – Isaiah 42:8 NIV

Prayer invites God into our lives to help us deal with emotional blocks and resistance from friends. His desire is for us is to live according to His word. We are to pray for God's Will to be done, which is linked to the confession of our sins to God, forgiving others as God has forgiven us, and acknowledging that "God will not test us beyond our ability to bear and will always provide a way out" (1 Corinthians 10:13). All of this and more, it is no wonder that we are to honor and set apart (i.e., to sanctify) His name for it is Holy.

> ***Hallowed Be Your Name,*** Lord, you are to be revered. Even your name is sacred. Help me hallow it – treating it as holy and sacred.
>
> –Timothy Jones,
> The Art of Prayer

We pray that God ***Our Father*** will be given the reverence and honor due to Him. The Holiness of God's Name testifies to His supreme authority to separate good judgment from evil, and the power of a spiritual life from an unworthy, profane, and flesh driven life. He is the creator of Earth and all living creatures and of places and things we have no knowledge of its good or bad. As children of God, we pray that we keep His name Holy to all people through our work and deeds.

> [22] Therefore say to the Israelites, This is what the Sovereign LORD says: It is not for your sake, people of Israel, that I am going to do these things, but for the sake of my holy name, which you have profaned among the nations where you have gone. [23] I will show the holiness of my great name, which has been profaned among the nations, the name you have profaned among them. Then the nations will know that I am the LORD, declares the Sovereign LORD, when I am proved holy through you before their eyes.
>
> – Ezekiel 36:22-23 NIV

The Meaning of Holiness

A person's name has always been more than just a name. It defines and represents everything about the person. The name of God stands for character and nature of His being, as He said in Exodus 3:14-15 NIV, [14] God said to Moses, "I AM WHO I AM. This is what you are to say to the Israelites: 'I AM has sent me to you.'" [15] God also said to Moses, "Say to the Israelites, 'The LORD, the God of your fathers – the God of Abraham, the God of Isaac and the God of Jacob – has sent me to you.' "This is my name forever, the name you shall call me from generation to generation." In this regards, according to J. I. Packer, "The *theological* word for this is God's *transcendence*, which means He exists apart from and not subject to the limitations of the material universe."

The point of all this lies in the incomprehensible fact that God is beyond what we think of as matter, space, and time. There are no limits placed on His Name and His Presence. God is beyond explanation. He is eternal, self-sustaining, and everlasting. As Peter Amsterdam says, "God's holiness is the essential difference between God

God is morally perfect in character and action. He is pure and righteous. He has no evil desires, motives, thoughts, words, or acts. He is eternally and unchangeably holy.

and man." Hence, we are to respect God's name for it is not of our world.

We must not use God's name casually or with vulgarity. God is Creator of everything. Man is the created. He is the creature and, thus God is superior to man and everything else in every way possible. God is perfect while man is imperfect. This point is critical in that it sets God apart from man's imperfections.

In Isaiah's vision of the Lord in the year that King Uzziah died, he spoke of the holiness of God: "I saw the Lord sitting upon a throne, high and lifted up; and the train of His robe filled the temple. Above Him stood the seraphim. Each had six wings: with two he covered his face, and with two he covered his feet, and with two he flew. And one called to another and said: 'Holy, holy, holy is the Lord of hosts; the whole earth is full of His glory!'"

God Cares For Us

The ways of man have been an exercise in futility, which has resulted in war, grief, and misery. Thus, trying to live without God is defined by our imperfections that lead to dissension, chaos, and eternal death. What God offers us is the opportunity to be with Him in Heaven. He made this possible through His Son, Jesus Christ who died on the cross for our sins. Jesus says in Matthew 6:33, "But seek ye first the kingdom of God, and his righteousness; and all these things shall be added unto you..." ***All these things*** include what we eat, what we drink, and what we wear (Matthew 6:25). Hence, there is no reason to be anxious about life because our sovereign Father in Heaven cares for us. Look at the birds and the lilies of the field. Birds have food to eat because God provides for them (Psalm 147:9). God sent His Son as light into the world that everyone who believes in Him may not remain in darkness.

> [44] Then Jesus cried out, "Whoever believes in me does not believe in me only, but in the one who sent me. [45] The one who looks at me is seeing the one who sent me. [46] I have come into the world as a light, so that no one who believes in me should stay in darkness."
>
> – John 12:44-46 NIV

Jesus, the Son of Man did not come to be served, but [28] "...to serve, and to give his life as a ransom for many." [29] As Jesus and his disciples were leaving Jericho, a large crowd followed him. [30] Two blind men were sitting by the roadside, and when they heard that Jesus was going by, they shouted, "Lord, Son of David, have mercy on us!" [31] The crowd rebuked them and told them to be quiet, but they shouted all the louder, "Lord, Son of David, have mercy on us!" [32] Jesus stopped and called them. "What do you want me to do for you?" he asked. [33] "Lord," they answered, "we want our sight." [34] Jesus had compassion on them and touched their eyes. Immediately they received their sight and followed him (Matthew 20:28-34 NIV).

"To serve" is the Will of God, as pointed out in John 6:40 NIV, "...that everyone who looks to the Son and believes in Him shall have eternal life...." God cares for us. He understands that we are stressed out and confused more than we are relaxed and clear headed. He understands that we need help in growing in spiritual maturity. He understands our disappointments and feelings of defeat. We are not alone. God loves us, and we must trust Him in faith until death, in the hope of the resurrection.

> "...I am with you always, to the close of the ages."
>
> – Matthew 28:20

When we pray ***Hallowed be Thy Name*** – God speaks to our hearts and invites us into His presence so that His Will is done on Earth as in Heaven. For God sent His son into the world to reconcile our sins by providing forgiveness of our sins. He invites us to share our needs and prayers with others. He helps each of us with our depressing and disappointing thoughts. His presence is always with us. Even when we don't cry out to God, He is with us. We simply have to open up to receive what He has to offer us. God may not change the circumstances we are in, but He will keep the circumstances from defeating and destroying us.

Chapter 4

Thy Kingdom Come

Daddy, what does "Thy Kingdom Come" mean? Well, son, it refers to the final coming of the reign of God through Christ's return.

THE KINGDOM OF God lies ahead of us when everything He has created has returned to God. Thus, when we say ***Thy Kingdom Come***, we understand it to mean **Christ Himself**, which is the coming of the reign of God through Christ's return. The Kingdom of God is linked to the church. That is why we are committed to the church, which is done by living and sharing God's message in our community, state, nation, and throughout the world.

By praying The Lord's Prayer, we keep the wheels of humanity moving in the direction of God's Kingdom in Heaven and His Will. Prayer keeps our eyes, ears, and hearts open to defeat the desire of Satan to engage the Battle of Wills with God. Through prayer we become part of a larger family to please God and to do His Will. While it is true we cannot do it as well as Jesus did for we are sinners in thoughts, deeds, and actions, He will help us through our prayers

Jesus said in Matthew 24:14 ESV,

"And this gospel of the kingdom will be proclaimed throughout the whole world as a testimony to all nations, and then the end will come."

to align our minds and actions with Him in anticipation of the 1000 year Millennium Kingdom.

> ***Let Us Look For The Good In The Bad:*** By faith our prayers are heard. God will deliver us from Satan. Thus, let us pray now, not later. Let us pray with feelings from the heart and love of God and His Son, Jesus Christ. Let us be grateful for all that God provides in our lives today, tomorrow, and forever.

With God's support and our support, individually and collectively, in fighting evil in this world, the power of Satan will give way to the existence of the Kingdom of the Lord Jesus Christ. His Kingdom will spread throughout the world with the belief that God rules the Earth and that it will be as Heaven.

God's love and forgiveness comes from praying for ***Thy Kingdom Come***. The shift from "it is all about me" to a communion with others will give rise to increased humility and shared hope and dreams. It is then that our understanding of prayer and the peace it brings will set the stage for a deeper personal spiritual experience and connection with Our Father in Heaven. It is the same as saying Lord I want your authority as Lord of Lords to be established in my life.

Now is the time to take up the faithful calling and the work of communion with Jesus Christ and His Father, God. The work that we do today will help each of us in the realization of the petition – ***Thy Kingdom Come***. It is what we are given to do when we pray. Why not look upon it as the transition from where we are presently to where we want to be. In other words, we move from a learned helplessness to a compassionate power of people in agreement with the will and desire of God.

The critical step is to engage others in this thinking so they will be able to work through their trials and tribulations in life. This process begins with prayer that provides the energy and means to helping ourselves and others close and far away to learn and live by faith in Jesus Christ.

> ***Key Points:*** Jesus called out, [46] Oh God, My God, why have you forsaken me? (Matt. 27:46) [34] Just before He died, Jesus prayed for his persecutors, "Forgive them for they know not what they do." (Luke 23:34) Then, [46] Jesus called out with a loud voice, "Father, into your hands I commit my spirit, and with that He gave up His spirit." (Luke 23:46)

Forgiveness of Sins

The crucifixion of Jesus Christ represents the supreme confirmation of God's plan of salvation and the coming of His Kingdom. The words that Jesus uttered confirmed the Holy Life that He lived, which ended with the gift of Himself in obedience to God, His Father. The gift of His life for the sins of the world is the ultimate act of God's love for us and His desire that we overcome our sinfulness.

But I tell you who hear me: Love your enemies, do good to those who hate you, bless those who curse you, pray for those who ill-treat you.

– Luke 6:27-28 GNT

Luke 23:43 helps us to understand that Heaven is offered to each person, regardless of age, financial status, or gender who places his or her trust in Jesus Christ. This point is supported by the fact that the reason Jesus came into this world was to give His life as a ransom for many (Mark 10:45). Thus, it was required that He suffer (Luke 24:26) so that he might make atonement for our sins and bring forgiveness to the world. Jesus said in Luke 24:46-47 GNT, [46] This is what is written: The Messiah will suffer and rise from the dead on the third day, [47] and repentance for the forgiveness of sins will be preached in his name to all nations, beginning at Jerusalem.

Seek First the Kingdom of God

To pray ***Thy Kingdom Come*** cannot be a prayer of the lips alone, but at the request of Jesus Christ to glorify His Father – God, His Kingdom, and God's work. It is a prayer of demonstration of our will as children of God to celebrate and support the awesome sacrifice of Jesus on the cross. Our hope is firm and steadfast when we "seek first the Kingdom of God" (Matthew 6:33 NIV), for in Jesus Christ the Son of God we have the forgiveness of sins and life forever in Heaven.

All Christians must share their love and the good news of redemption and their inability to solve life's problems without the presence of God and His Kingdom on Earth. This is most evident by the two World Wars and millions of deaths during the 20th century. It is hard to imagine but true that we have been almost perpetually at war with each other for decades. Clearly, this point is not new. Jeremiah explains the problem with human reasoning apart from God.

> "O LORD, I know the way of man is not in himself, it is not in man who walks to direct his own steps."
>
> – Jeremiah 10:23 NKJV

Without God and His Kingdom, the human race does not know how to govern itself. It cannot make good decisions about life's problems. The book of Proverbs tells us, "There is a way that seems right to a man, but its end is the way of death" (Proverbs 14:12 NKJV). Earlier, through the prophet Isaiah, God told ancient Israel: [2] But your iniquities have separated you from your God; your sins have hidden his face from you, so that he will not hear. [3] For your hands are stained with blood, your fingers with guilt. Your lips have spoken falsely, and your tongue mutters wicked things. [4] No one calls for justice; no one pleads a case with integrity. They rely on empty arguments, they utter lies; they conceive trouble and give birth to evil (Isaiah 59:2-4 NKJV).

In Isaiah 59:13-15 NIV, the prophet continued to describe the progression that takes place when God is rejected by mankind due to their selfish desires, [13] ...rebellion and treachery against the LORD, turning our backs on our God, inciting revolt and oppression, uttering lies our hearts have conceived. [14] So justice is driven back, and righteousness stands at a distance; truth has stumbled in the streets, honesty cannot enter. [15] Truth is nowhere to be found, and whoever shuns evil becomes a prey. The LORD looked and was displeased that there was no justice.

And in the days of those kings shall the God of heaven set up a kingdom which shall never be destroyed, nor shall the sovereignty thereof be left to another people; but it shall break in pieces and consume all these kingdoms, and it shall stand for ever.

– Daniel 2:44

To seek first the Kingdom of God means that we must be eager to embrace and glorify God. We need God to help us avoid sin and violence. Consequently, this means that the Kingdom of God, under the direction of His Son, Jesus Christ and His return to Earth, must be established to save man from himself. This point is highlighted in Revelation 11:15 NIV, [15] The seventh angel sounded his trumpet, and there were loud voices in Heaven, which said "The Kingdom of the world has become the Kingdom of our Lord and of His Messiah, and He will reign forever and ever."

Jesus Christ told Nicodemus that we must be "born again" (John 3:3). This means that entering the Kingdom of God begins with baptism, which signifies the death of the former sinful person and the beginning of a ***new life*** dedicated to Jesus Christ.

> [1] What shall we say, then? Shall we go on sinning so that grace may increase? [2] By no means! We died to sin; how can we live in it any longer? [3] Or don't you know that all of us who were baptized into Christ Jesus were baptized into his death? [4] We were therefore buried with him through baptism into death in order that, just as Christ was raised from the dead through the glory of the Father, we too may live a new life. [5] If we have been united with him like this in his death, we will certainly also be united with him in his resurrection.
>
> – Romans 6:1-5 NIV

The ***New Life*** is also met with questions such as: What about meeting my financial needs? Where will my food and drink come from? Will I have a place to sleep? The answer to each question is found in what Jesus said in Matthew 6:33, "Seek ye first the Kingdom of God, and his righteousness; and all these things shall be added unto you." Seek the Kingdom of God, especially given the truths of Solomon who said in Proverbs 14:12 NKJV that, "there is a way that seems right to a man, but its end is the way of death" and as well Jeremiah 10:23 NKJV who said, "O LORD, I know the way of man is not in himself; it is not in man who walks to direct his own steps."

How? By repentance and belief in Jesus Christ and the doors will open by which entrance into this glorious Kingdom will be permitted. Why, as written in Romans 3:23, "…For all have sinned, and come short of the glory of God." Romans 6:23 adds that "the wages of sin is death, but the gift of God is eternal life in Christ Jesus our Lord." Thus, it is imperative that society changes how it thinks if it is going to move away from sin to keeping God's commandments.

This point is further emphasized in Matthew 19:17 when Jesus said, "...but if thou wilt enter into life, keep the commandments."

The Holy Spirit and Baptism

Baptism requires the laying on of hands. This is believed necessary to receive the Holy Spirit (Acts 19:6), which is what makes one an actual child of God. When we pray ***Thy Kingdom Come,*** we are also praying for the reign of the kingdom of God in our lives (Luke 17:21). When we are under God's rule, and when He is in control of our lives, we are living the Kingdom of God. As Romans 14:17 NKJV says, it is not rules and regulations, but "righteousness and peace and joy in the Holy Spirit".

Once a person has the Holy Spirit, that person has Christ in him or her (Colossians 1:27). God offers us the gift of forgiveness of our sins and the gift of the indwelling presence of God's Holy Spirit through baptism, which makes possible the gift of God, which is eternal life in Christ Jesus our Lord (Romans 6:23). Baptism symbolizes our faith: [3] "...that Jesus Christ died for our sins in accordance with the Scriptures, [4] that He was buried, and that He was raised on the third day in accordance with the scriptures" (1 Corinthians 15:3-4).

When we repent of our sins and we keep God's commandments, the next step is baptism.

The immersion (baptism) is an acknowledgement of the need for our old sinful way of life to be put away and buried forever. The rising from the water symbolizes the first steps in our newness of life. Through baptism we are united with God to live a new Christian life. It is a change from flesh and blood to immortality. Baptism reminds us that even though we have sinned, God makes us clean and fills us with the Holy Spirit.

Paul said in 2 Corinthians 5:17 NKJV, "If anyone is in Christ, he is a new creation; the old has gone, the new has come!" Baptism is God's way of marking us as part of His new creation and as members of His covenant. Now that we know what the Kingdom of God is on Earth, we need to "…seek the Kingdom of God and His righteousness…" (Matthew 6:33 NKJV). This means that although we are interested in doing what is necessary to live a good life on Earth, we are more interested in what God wants us to do. This is true even more so when we are faced with a series of problem-solving opportunities.

The problems we face will either defeat us or develop us. It all depends on how we respond to problems we experience at work, home, and in our communities. Unfortunately, most people fail to see the "good in the bad". The problem is they are not trusting the Holy Spirit to help them do the right thing in response to, for example, losing their job due to a colleague's remarks. Thus, there is the possibility of failing to respond appropriately. Yet, according to the scriptures, the Holy Spirit abides with every person who believes in Jesus Christ as the Son of God. The Holy Spirit is a counselor and source of peace.

The Holy Spirit will assist us during times of distress for, as Benny Hinn says, "God does not intend for you to stray from the path He has set for you to follow. He did not create you to see you fail." That's why you should not become unduly alarmed when facing life's problems. After all, as strange as it might sound, problems often point us in a new direction and motivate us to change or to think differently. Our problems may be the work of God to get our attention or to test our faith.

> [2] Consider it pure joy, my brothers and sisters, whenever you face trials of many kinds, [3] because you know that the testing of your faith produces perseverance.
>
> – James 1:2-3 NIV

We know that the testing of our faith renders us stronger. We are eager to pray to ***Our Father*** and ***Thy Kingdom Come.*** The Holy Spirit makes it possible to express our thoughts and concerns, however difficult it might be. All we need to do is ask for help by saying, "Teach me how to pray so that I will learn from my trials."

[3] Not only that, but we rejoice in our sufferings, knowing that suffering produces endurance, [4] and endurance produces character, and character produces hope.

– Romans 5:3-4 ESV

Also, remember that a problem at work may be a blessing, especially when the Holy Spirit is helping us to bear witness with our spirit that we are children of God. In fact, we should be happy when we have problems because they build our character and help us to grow in our hope of eternal life. God is at work in our lives even when we feel disconnected or at a total loss with the world.

Thus, we pray: "Thank you Jesus for when you return, you are going to take us home. We belong to you for you paid the price on Calvary. Amen." Jesus gives us the strength to live with a smile while the Holy Spirit gives us the rest we need. A close relationship in prayer with the Holy Spirit means that we will have closer relationship with Jesus Christ and ***Our Father in Heaven.***

When we pray, we speak to God. When we pray, Jesus prays in us.

[16] Rejoice always, [17] pray continually, [18] give thanks in all circumstances; for this is God's will for you in Christ Jesus. [19] Do not quench the Spirit.

– 1 Thessalonians 5:16-19 NIV

The petition, ***Thy Kingdom Come***, in The Lord's Prayer has two important objectives. First, we are asking that while we are living on Earth, we experience honesty and love from each and every person we encounter. The second objective is that we pray for the Kingdom of God's existence on Earth at the end of time and that He grants us eternal life.

> [1] Now there was a man of the Pharisees named Nicodemus, a ruler of the Jews. [2] This man came to Jesus by night and said to him, "Rabbi, we know that you are a teacher come from God, for no one can do these signs that you do unless God is with him." [3] Jesus answered him, "Truly, truly, I say to you, unless one is born again he cannot see the Kingdom of God." [4] Nicodemus said to him, "How can a man be born when he is old? Can he enter a second time into his mother's womb and be born?" [5] Jesus answered, "Truly, truly, I say to you, unless one is born of water and the Spirit, he cannot enter the Kingdom of God."
>
> – John 3:1-5 NKJV

According to Brant Pitre, this is why many scholars have stated that ***Thy Kingdom Come*** is "arguably the heart not only of The Lord's Prayer, but of Jesus' entire mission and message." Not surprisingly, then, this petition ties all of Scripture together. As Christians, God asks that we "…act justly, love tenderly, and walk humbly with our God" (Micah 6:8). We pray for ***Thy Kingdom Come*** sooner than later. We pray that God will help us create communities and work places where we:

- Will act justly;
- Will be helpers without bitterness;
- Will forgive our imperfect friends and colleagues who victimize us;

- Will empower those who are dependent on others for their participation in everyday events;
- Learn to avoid pushing things off instead of taking the time to walk humbly with everyone; and
- Will stop the victimization of the poor so that everyone has enough food, clean water and air, access to education, and the essentials for a healthy life.

Chapter 5

Thy Will Be Done on Earth as It Is in Heaven

> God wants you to do His will.... He cleansed you of your sins by sending His Son Jesus to die for you, and He sent the Holy Spirit into you, planting His own nature within you. All that is required is for you to surrender yourself to Him by an act of your will and come under His sovereignty, where His will is done on earth as it is in heaven.
>
> – Everett L. Fullam

WE PRAY THE petition, ***Thy Will Be Done on Earth as It Is in Heaven***, asking for God's grace to help us to do His will on Earth. We pray that we will desire less of our will and more of His will be done. We pray that God brings His will so that we may experience and share Heaven on Earth. This thinking is believed to be consistent with our purpose, which is not to do our will but rather the will of God as pointed out by Jesus in Matthew 22:37-39 ESV: [37] You shall love the Lord your God with all your heart and with all your soul and with all your mind. [38] This is the first and greatest commandment. [39] And the second is like it: You shall love your neighbor as yourself. Thus, it is important that we devote ourselves to doing God's will and serving God the way He wishes, whether it is at home, work, or wherever.

Children of God

We are sent by God to inspire (2 Peter 1:20-21), instruct (Acts 1:2), transform (Acts 2:41), and work miracles (John 14:12). Hence, God's purpose for creating human beings is for them to become members of His family and to live with Him forever in Heaven. This point is illustrated in Christ's background and reason for coming in the flesh. John 1:10-14 NKJV says, "He was in the world, and the world was made through Him, and the world did not know Him. He came to His own, and His own did not receive Him. But as many as received Him, to them He gave the right to become children of God, to those who believe in His name: who were born, not of blood, nor of the will of the flesh, nor of *the will of man, but of God*."

To become children of God, we must pray God's will be done on Earth as it is in Heaven. We must listen and discern what we feel His will is in our lives. It is through our prayer that we learn to trust that God is at work in us. We learn to sense God's purpose in our lives, and if we want to do something that is not in God's will we learn that as well. As Romans 12:2 ESV says, "Do not be conformed to this world, but be transformed by the renewal of your mind, that by testing you may discern what is the will of God, what is good and acceptable and perfect."

To fail to embrace ***Thy Will Be Done on Earth as It Is in Heaven*** is not an option. Dr. Myles Munroe says, "God's plan is for man to desire what He desires, to will what He wills, and to ask Him to accomplish His purposes in the world so that goodness and truth may reign on the Earth rather than evil and darkness." Just as Jesus Christ delivered us from the power of sin, the backbone of our prayers is our support of God's purpose and will. This raises the question: Are you willing to help God to fulfill ***Thy Will Be Done on Earth as It Is in Heaven?*** If so, there is an excellent chance that every good thing of yours and every act driven by your faith will be fulfilled.

If any man will come after me, let him deny himself, and take up his cross daily, and follow me.

– Luke 9:23

We must place God's Kingdom and purpose above our needs and wants. We do this in prayer with the desire to know what God wants us to do. By placing God's Kingdom before our needs, we help to ensure that "God's Will" be done on Earth. This is how we should pray and how it should be. It is the Christians' responsibility to share with love our spiritual and material goods. Thus, we pray that the will of God may be done. Why? Because by faith we believe that "His Will" is perfect love and justice. It is His desire that no one should perish but have everlasting life in Heaven. But, the difficulty is in solving the problem of sin.

Since God is all-powerful, why do we need to pray for His will to be done? Is it because Jesus is using The Lord's Prayer to help us align our thinking with God's purpose and His plans for us? His Will is what is important and, therefore, it must come before our will. ***God's Will*** is that every human being becomes part of His family in Heaven. This means that we must embrace His Son, Jesus Christ. All who believe in Him, repent their sins, and be baptized will receive the Holy Spirit from which we are converted and saved forever to live in Heaven. Again, this is the Will of God.

> ***Think For A Moment.*** *Do you have an understanding or a feeling of how God is using your current life circumstances to prepare you for a great calling?*

Furthering His Kingdom

To recognize the sovereignty of God over everything is a way of saying, "Thank you God for having this world under your control, not mine!" After all, God knows what is best for us. If we live according to God's Will, we will have peace in knowing that the One who taught us to pray ***Thy Will Be Done on Earth as It Is in Heaven*** has our lives in His hands.

Pray that God's grace and His Spirit will guide us into conformity with His.

Understandably, while it is acceptable for us to tell God what our will is for a given situation, we should always defer in prayer to God's Will above our will. Jesus did this in the Garden of Gethsemane when He was facing torture and death on the cross: "…he fell with his face to the ground and prayed, 'My Father, if it is possible, may this cup be taken from me. Yet not as I will, but as you will'" (Matthew 26:39 NIVUK).

David Treybig said, "God's will for us is that we gradually change from humans with natural, human actions and ways of thinking, which are not in harmony with God's laws, to people who think and act like God." Hence, when we say ***Thy Will Be Done on Earth as It Is in Heaven***, we are asking God to set the stage for loving one another as I have loved you (John 13:34).

Given the world events, suffering, and disappointments, it isn't easy to develop a state of mind that is driven by thoughts of doing God's will. Too often we are poised to be equally as mean or bad. Yet, regardless of the state of personal conflict and pain, we must pray to God that His will be done on earth as it is in Heaven. As human beings we are without the strength, knowledge, and purpose to survive without God's mercy and grace. We need God's help. When we pray "***Thy Will Be Done***"

We look to and trust God for our basic necessities of life each and every day.

we are asking for God's involvement in our lives according to His purpose.

> As a Christian, we believe this because we "Trust God". Belief and trust are the keys to an unquestioning faith in Jesus Christ. "Trust in the Lord forever, for the LORD, the LORD, is the Rock eternal."
>
> – Isaiah 26:4 NIV

We need God in our lives or otherwise we will become slaves to Satan. We need God to take control of how we think and what we do. That is why each person must surrender to God's spirit, power, and opportunity to live in a close personal relationship with Him. Our needs must be viewed in the context of God's Will. Hence, we pray that His Will be done on Earth as it is in Heaven.

The apostle Paul wrote in Ephesians 4:32 that we should "Become kind to one another, tenderly compassionate, freely forgiving one another just as God also by Christ freely forgave you." ***Thy Will Be Done on Earth as It Is in Heaven*** also extends to the ***10 Commandments*** that were given by God from Mount Sinai to show us how to live and please Him forever. Moses recorded God's words in Exodus 20:1-26 and, then, recounted the event again in Deuteronomy 5:1-22, which are:

1. I, the Lord, am your God. You shall not have other gods before me.
2. You shall not make idols.
3. You shall not take the name of the Lord God in vain.
4. Remember to keep holy the Lord's Day.
5. Honor your father and your mother.
6. You shall not kill.
7. You shall not commit adultery.

8. You shall not steal.
9. You shall not bear false witness against your neighbor.
10. You shall not covet your neighbor's goods.

During His ministry on Earth, one of the scribes asked Jesus, "Which is the first commandment of all?" [37] Jesus replied: "Love the Lord your God with all your heart and with all your soul and with all your mind. [38] This is the first and greatest commandment. [39] And the second is like it: Love your neighbor as yourself. [40] All the Law and the Prophets hang on these two commandments" (Matthew 22:37-40 NIV). It is imperative that we do not violate the first and second laws.

> ***Key Point:*** The Kingdom of God exists on Earth when God's Will is done, thus someday Earth will be as Heaven and everyone who believes in Jesus as the Son of God will live there.

To pray ***Thy Will Be Done on Earth as It Is in Heaven*** is to declare our desire and willingness to live in accordance with the Will of God on Earth as faithfully as the Angels and Saints do in Heaven. Also, it is a powerful expression of faith that is in agreement with what the Christian apostle John wrote in Revelation, "[3] And I heard a great voice out of heaven saying, Behold, the tabernacle of God is with men, and he will dwell with them, and they shall be his people, and God himself shall be with them, and be their God.[4] And God shall wipe away all tears from their eyes; and there shall be no more death, neither sorrow, nor crying, neither shall there be any more pain: for the former things are passed away. [5] And he that sat upon the throne said, Behold, I make all things new. And he said unto me, Write: for these words are true and faithful" (Revelation 21:3-5).

By accepting in faith John's words, we acknowledge the belief that

God's Will is the means to ruling Earth, and that Earth will be as Heaven. We are blessed to live as Christians with God in our hearts and minds on Earth, thus helping to bring about the transition of Heaven on Earth in our own lives and those with whom we come into contact with. This means we are agents of change with the mission to share the good news of God's love for humanity with everyone we can, so that the world will be more like God's Kingdom.

Chapter 6

Give Us This Day Our Daily Bread

> We are focusing … on everything we need to live this day and do what we have been called to do today. We focus on this day only and let go of the struggles of the past and trust that God has tomorrow managed.
>
> – Frederick D. Maurice

WHILE THE FOURTH petition refers to bread as food for the body, it is also everything that makes up a person's life. This petition, ***Give Us This Day Our Daily Bread***, addresses the air we breathe, the wind in our face, the food we eat, the health we enjoy, and the basic necessities of our everyday lives. Our Father in Heaven gives us the "spiritual bread of life".

When we pray for our daily bread, we are asking God for the fullness of the Holy Spirit and the Lord Jesus that satisfy the heart of each of us.

Jesus taught the disciples this prayer because it glorifies God who provides us with personal, social, and economic blessings. Moreover, Jesus said, "I am the bread of life. He who comes to me will never go hungry, and whoever believes in me will never be thirsty" (John 6:35 NIV). We are His children and He is our God. For this reason, it is also about going to Jesus in prayer, being with Him in a spiritual connection with God the bread of life that holds the promise of eternity.

Ask and It Will be Given to You

With bold confidence, we turn to the Holy Spirit to help us pray to our Father in Heaven. It is there we grasp tightly our lifeline to eternity, knowing that while on Earth the gift of The Lord's Prayer provides both material and spiritual food. Thus, when we say ***Give Us This Day Our Daily Bread***, our prayer is in accordance with our everyday concerns of living. As children of Heaven, our Heavenly Father gives us the power and the strength that confirms our faith and belief in prayer. This we know is true because the Savior taught us in Matthew 7:7-8 to BSB, "Ask and it will be given to you; seek and you will find; knock and the door will be opened to you. For everyone who asks receives; he who seeks finds; and to him who knocks, the door will be opened."

> Let Us Pray
> Gracious God, we come before you, asking you to feed our hearts and souls and minds with food that you alone can provide and that you alone can satisfy. In our loneliness, in our despair, in our emptiness, in our shattered dreams, in our broken hearts, in our sin, in our separation from loved ones…Lord, you alone can fill those empty places. Feed us, O God, the One who has revealed himself as the Bread of Life.
> AMEN
>
> – Rev. Dr. Mark S. White

When we ask, seek, and knock in prayer according to God's will, Christians believe the door of answers and opportunities will be opened by our Heavenly Father. Equally important is the understanding that not all "asking, seeking, and knocking" will produce the result we want. Why? Because in all likelihood, too many of our prayers are more about what we personally want rather than praying for God's Kingdom and His Will be done in our lives. God knows best what we need and when we need it.

Without a request, it cannot be granted. If you do not seek, you will not find, and the door will not open if you do not knock.

Also, a prayer today and maybe another prayer three weeks or three months from now on behalf of something or an occasional annual asking for help from a bad situation may not be successful in opening the prayer door as when the same person prays day after day for God's will to be done on Earth in the lives of all who need Him. Prayers are meant to be about the needs of our parents, children, brothers, sisters, friends, and anyone who needs God's blessing. Praying for our daily bread is about love and compassion for others as well as for our own personal needs.

Prayer Changes Us

To pray is to make a personal connection with God. To pray daily with your heart open to God's Will is to promote a relationship with Him. The truth is that God wants a relationship with each of us. That is why He sent His Son, Jesus Christ, who lived a sinless life and who sacrificed His life on the cross for the sins of humankind. He wants us to walk with Him, to love Him, and to trust Him.

To pray The Lord's Prayer is to desire a close relationship with God and His Kingdom. The more we pray and read about prayer the closer we become to ***Our Father in Heaven***. Prayer changes us so that we can appreciate the significance of the petition – ***Give Us This Day***

Our Daily Bread. In short, it acknowledges that we may take all our needs to God.

> Whatever your need is — physical, emotional, relational, or spiritual — God will take care of it if you will depend on him. Pray today, "Give us this day our daily bread," and trust God to provide for you in every way.
>
> –Rick Warren

Interestingly, given the structure of the fourth petition, ***Give Us This Day Our Daily Bread***, it is important and necessary to pray daily, praying in faith that God will provide for our daily needs. In asking for our daily spiritual food, we acknowledge our walk in faith and our dependence on God and our desire for a relationship with God.

Jesus said, "I am the bread of life."

– John 6:35

Here, it is important to mention the word "our" in the sense of being dependent on God, thus highlighting the fact that all of us are subject to His guidance and will. This point is highlighted by Fr. Robin Ryan who said, "As we reflect on this petition for our daily bread, I would suggest that we come before God and honestly present our needs to him. What is it that you need right now in order to continue and grow in your life as a follower of Jesus?"

No matter how sophisticated we become in spiritual life, we still need regularly to come to God and tell God everything – the whole works – and allow God to be there with us and for us. Pouring out our spiritual needs to God in this honest way enables us to perceive the reality of God's presence in our lives. In your dialogue with the Lord, ask for the bread that you need to sustain you at that moment in time. Speak very concretely to God to be with your every step. As you do so, remember Jesus Christ and give your cares and your life to His Father in Heaven who loves you now and forever.

Placing Our Trust in God

The prayer for daily bread awakens the means to understanding what it is that we are asking of God. Jesus is saying that we need to turn to God daily, one day at a time. We need God to help give us the understanding and faith that without His presence in our lives we have no life at all. Also, we need to acknowledge that God has a legitimate claim on every person on the face of the earth, and that every talent we have should be used to highlight God's purpose in our lives.

> [31] So do not worry, saying, 'What shall we eat?' or 'What shall we drink?' or 'What shall we wear?' [32] For the pagans run after all these things, and your heavenly Father knows that you need them. [33] But seek first his kingdom and his righteousness, and all these things will be given to you as well. [34] Therefore do not worry about tomorrow, for tomorrow will worry about itself. Each day has enough trouble of its own.
>
> – Matthew 6:31-34 NIV

While it is clear that we need the mental and physical nourishment that comes from regular exercise, we also need spiritual nourishment such as when we are, "nourished on the truths of the faith…" (1 Timothy 4:6). In short, the Bible is meant to be food to Christians. Yet, it is common for Christians to feel spiritually thirsty and hungry. Strangely enough, we can even experience this feeling after we have read or studied the Bible. Why is that when we do not want to worry about tomorrow? Why can't we simply concentrate on seeking first God's Kingdom and His Righteousness?

We can believe this is so, given the context of Deuteronomy 8:17-18 NIV that challenged the concept of a self sufficient culture: [17] You may say to yourself, "My power and the strength of my hands have produced this wealth for me." [18] But remember the LORD your God, for it is he who gives you the ability to produce wealth, and so confirms his covenant, which he swore to your ancestors, as it is today. In other words, you have the ability to provide for your family. Where does that ability come from? God!

> Because of Jesus Christ, our Intercessor, we have the great privilege to pray directly to ***Our Father in Heaven*** to exhort us to not "worry about tomorrow, for tomorrow will worry about itself" (Matthew 6:34 NIV).

God waits for us to place our faith in His power. If you are a child of God, then, you can pray about anything. [6] Do not be anxious about anything, but in every situation, by prayer and petition, with thanksgiving, present your requests to God (Philippians 4:6 NIV). Submit yourselves therefore to God, and remember that daily bread does not refer just to food. God is our provider. He provides our daily bread of physical and spiritual health, mental well-being, positive thoughts and ideas, safe housing, good friends, happy marriage, healthy children, and a good government that sustains us so that we can do what we have been called to do today. Note that the request is not for material

[32] Jesus said to them, "Very truly I tell you, it is not Moses who has given you the bread from heaven, but it is my Father who gives you the true bread from heaven."

– John 6:32 NIV

wealth, but rather what is needed to be in harmony with what God expects of us on Earth.

> Our Heavenly Father,
> Today, I pray for all that is necessary for our soul and body. Thank you, Lord for I will focus on this day only and let go of the struggles of the past and trust You to take care of tomorrow. I pray in the name of Your Son, Jesus Christ, who died on the cross for our sins so that we may have eternal life in Heaven.
> Amen.

In John 6:35-40 NIV, [35] ...Jesus declared, "I am the bread of life. Whoever comes to me will never go hungry, and whoever believes in me will never be thirsty. [36] But as I told you, you have seen me and still you do not believe. [37] All those the Father gives me will come to me, and whoever comes to me I will never drive away. [38] For I have come down from heaven not to do my will but to do the will of Him who sent me. [39] And this is the will of Him who sent me that I shall lose none of all those he has given me, but raise them up at the last day. [40] For my Father's will is that everyone who looks to the Son and believes in him shall have eternal life, and I will raise them up at the last day."

Give Us This Day Our Daily Bread is the fourth of the seven petitions. The first three address God while the second four petitions are about our physical, spiritual, and mental needs. Each need is important, thus praying many times daily is required for our spiritual well-being on Earth. We pray for ***Our Daily Bread*** that teaches us to be closer to God for we are beholden to His mercy. We learn in the process of God's daily supply of grace to extend ourselves to others, especially to forgive others and their profane language and unkind criticism when we understand how much God has forgiven us.

> ***Key Point:*** Asking for our daily bread does not mean that we pray The Lord's Prayer and, then, sit back and do nothing. It is our responsibility to work for our basic necessities of life. But, it does mean that we can trust God to provide us a gift of what we need today so that we may glorify Our Father in Heaven.

Living a Day at a Time

> ***Give Us Today Our Daily Bread*** **that we be given the insight and faith to recognize that without God we have no life at all.**
>
> **– Bob Hansel**

This petition is about asking God for "this day's bread" that, in general, has nothing to do with the need of bread per se (although, biblically, bread is a synonym for food). It represents our daily needs that may be the need to vent our hostility toward a friend, to laugh when all else seems to have failed, to hold close a family member, to deal with an illness when there seems to be no answers, to pray for help, to let go of fear and loneliness, to handle heartbreak, and so on.

Tomorrow, when we pray again for our daily bread, it may be that we pray for God to be with us, to help and direct our thinking, and to help us look for the good in people. Hence, in this way, through prayer, we learn to be grateful and filled with happiness for the physical, emotional, and spiritual nourishment of God's presence. God will not fail to provide love to us, and we should not go to sleep without telling those we love that we love them. Hence, it is as Bob Hansel said, "...what we're asking is that God would enter each day into our very being, giving us the Spirit of peace and power, without which there is no life worth living."

> ***Key Point:*** Pray quietly and regularly. The prayerful realization of the presence of God is a personal, living experience here and now.

Chapter 7

Forgive Us Our Debts as We Forgive Our Debtors

Jesus said that we are to love our enemies, bless them that curse us, do good to them that hate us, and pray for them which despitefully use us and persecute us. And He added that if we do this, we may be the children of our Father which is in Heaven, "for he makes his sun to rise on the evil and on the good, and sends rain on the just and on the unjust."

– Matthew 5:44-45

FORGIVING SOMEONE IS often the hardest thing a person can do. Yet, Jesus said to the disciples in Matthew 6:14-15 ESV, [14]…if you forgive others their trespasses, your heavenly Father will also forgive you, [15]but if you do not forgive others their trespasses, neither will your Father forgive your trespasses. Forgiveness is therefore a critical part of the Christian's life. God will not forgive us of our debts as long as we live in an unforgiving state of mind. The message is simple. Look for the good in the bad and get over the hurt.

Pope John Paul II reminds us: "Forgiveness is the key to peace."

Hardly anyone will go through life without being hurt and disappointed by a family member, friend, or a colleague. The world is made up of people who live to take advantage of others. It may mean telling a lie or making up a story about a family member or a friend. Many people will not think twice about taking advantage of a friend. It is as if they believe what they are doing or have done is okay. They may think there is nothing wrong with their actions and/or behaviors, especially since: "... for they know not what they do" (Luke 23:34).

However difficult it is, we must forgive those who have wronged us so we can live a happier life on Earth with God here and in Heaven. Forgiveness is an expression of faith in our relationship with Jesus Christ and Our Father, God. The moment we forgive those who sin against us, the power of that sin over our lives is removed. It is then we are free from being further damaged by the sin. Forgiveness turns the hurt into a higher power of love, understanding, and reconciliation.

> ***Key Point:*** We need forgiveness to be happy. We need forgiveness to be mentally healthy.
>
> – Elmer L. Towns

When we pray to God, "Our Father" we are in communion with him and his Son, Jesus Christ. We ask for an outpouring of His mercy on behalf of our sins with the understanding that we have forgiven those who have trespassed against us. If we have not forgiven the sins of our debtors, God will not forgive us for our debts. We cannot expect forgiveness if we are not willing to forgive and love those who sin against us.

Failure to Please God

The Lord's Prayer provides us the opportunity to stand before God and pray even though we fail time after time in doing the things that please God. As sinners, we fail to pray with meaning. We fail in pleasing God because we are greedy, violent, and self-centered. As God's children, we fail to understand the urgency of our need for forgiveness even though "the wages of sin is death" (Romans 6:23 NIV). God is willing to take away our sin (John 1:29). But, first, we must confess our sins, and then He is faithful and just to forgive us our sins, and to cleanse us from all unrighteousness (John 1:9).

Ask and it will be given to you; seek, and you will find; knock, and it will be opened to you. For everyone who asks, receives, and one who seeks finds, and to one who knocks it will be opened.

– Luke 11:9-10 NIV

The next step, once again, is that we need to forgive those who hurt us, rejected us, and disappointed us. We must forgive them for the wrong they have done to us and our families. We must stop thinking about "paying them back" for what they took from us, regardless of whether it was rape, physical abuse, or emotional abuse. We must not take revenge, for it is written: "It is mine to avenge; I will repay, says the Lord" (Romans 12:19 NIV). While despising those who hurt us is understandable and even expected at times, we cannot grow in Christ when hatred is at the center of our thoughts. That is why we pray that God will forgive us of our sins as we forgive those who have sinned against us.

> ***Key Point:*** The high cost of mentally and emotionally dealing with the desire to get even is in God's hands. We are forgiven our debts as we forgive our debtors and move on!

After all, do you really want to live however long as possible with hate and bitterness constantly on your mind? Such a state of existence is unhealthy in itself. It is certainly not living a Christian life. Not being able to let go of the pain of the past destroys everything that is good in the present. Christ paid in full for our sins, and we must be forthcoming in forgiving the sins of others.

Regardless of the hurt, pain, and disappointment of a close friend, freedom comes with forgiving his or her trespasses against us. As Colossians 3:13 NIV says, we must "Bear with each other and forgive one another if any of you has a grievance against someone. Forgive as the Lord forgave you." The fact that we ask God for forgiveness also acknowledges Our Father's power and primacy.

- Let us pray for broken relationships and friendships that we know exist, not for retribution.
- Let us acknowledge the good life that comes from increased awareness and gratitude for knowing that life goes on.
- Let us be thankful that forgiveness allows us to stop being controlled by painful memories and wounds of the past.
- Let us be grateful that we have through prayer and forgiveness a credible means to letting go of the anger and resentment.
- Let us acknowledge that God will make things right.

Understanding Forgiveness

Faith is critical to understanding forgiveness, resentment, and the desire for revenge. While it is natural to feel angry, revenge puts you on the same level as the person who hurt you. To thrive as a spiritual person, faith is the turning point in giving someone another chance – especially when a colleague has fallen short of being a true friend. However, to forgive someone of doing a great injustice to you or your family does not mean that you automatically turn a blind eye to it.

Before you embark on a journey of revenge, dig two graves.

– Confucius

It is understandable that we should remember the anger that results from the conditions of something that created devastating events and/or emotions. Those who caused the hurt are still responsible for their behavior and the negative effects on a person's life, his/her health, and well-being. That person will have to live with the betrayal of a friend, family member, or colleague.

> Forgive the man who sins, but condemn the evil itself. We must aid the man, but abhor and oppose the evil which we think he has. Love your enemies, pray for them that despitefully use you and persecute you.
>
> – Hugo Lj. Odhner

Forgiveness is not excusing or condoning acts of violence. There are right and wrong ways of interacting with other human beings. When an act of violence is intentional, it is right that the person responsible is held accountable. This is not revenge or hatred towards the person. Rather, it is society's way of unburdening itself from the pain of someone hurting another person. Once that person understands his or her actions hurt someone else and is placed in jail, it helps with finding some degree of peace. It also helps in remembering the injustice and hurt in a different way, thus allowing for the "moving on" to become a little easier.

More often than not, to let go of the hurt created by the greedy exploitations of friends and colleagues is a state of mind that requires spiritual boldness. Faith in Jesus Christ as the Son of God is the bridge to forgiveness, which is empowered by prayer. The truth is that we must pray daily for forgiveness to move closer to God. When we do this in faith that our prayers will be

Resentment is like drinking poison and then hoping it will kill your enemies.

– Nelson Mandela

answered, it releases us from unhappiness and separation from God. We do this because we are instructed to do so in The Lord's Prayer. We pray for the forgiveness of our sins so that we might experience the healing power of forgiveness from God. Also, we pray about forgiving ourselves for the self-inflicted injuries we have done so that we can live without the bitterness and resentment. After all, we are not perfect. We all make mistakes.

> ***Key Point:*** The problem is that it is difficult to forgive or to turn a blind eye to certain acts of unkindness or envy. This is why we need God's help, and He gives it. It is also the reason we can pray for those who have mistreated or hurt us.

Liberation

The healing power of forgiveness lies in setting others free so that we are sat free from the resentment and the negative feelings that result when we are deeply hurt. Only then is it likely that we will let go of the emotional hurt and suffering and move forward with life without the experiences of the past dominating the future. This is consistent with Matthew 5:44 regarding the Lord's teachings in the Sermon on the Mount: "Do good to them that hate you, and pray for them which despitefully use you." Forgiveness comes down to faith in God and trust in His Son, Jesus Christ, who died on the cross for our sins.

God's forgiveness of us is contingent on our forgiveness of others.

Forgiveness is not about forgetting about the pain and rage that comes with mistreatment. Rather, it is about making the decision to let go of the anger, rage, and the anxiety. With Faith in God, we can forgive others when we are hurt even when we may never know why some things happen in life.

But, clearly, our job is to stay the course of enduring the worst of humanity if that is in our future. This insight into not holding a grudge is important, especially since every bad thing that happens to us prepares us to start the healing process and move closer to God. Therefore, as difficult as it is to accept that every hurtful situation should move us to forgive, let us remember that we need to forgive to be forgiven.

Getting rid of the negative feelings, the disappointments, and the blatant acts of abuse is the key to better mental and physical health. Being willing to forgive the inevitable conflicts with others in life is associated with a lower heart rate and blood pressure as well as an overall decrease in the work of the heart. Mentally speaking, it is liberating to know that we can forgive and move on with life no matter how we have been wronged and mistreated.

Nothing good comes from not casting the burden or resentment upon Christ within us. Forgiveness is freedom to be at peace inside one's own mind and body that allows for improved sleep and quality of life. Life is too short not to forgive. This understanding is the ultimate liberation that is God's will and expectation from each of us.

> To forgive is to set a prisoner free and discover that the prisoner was you.
>
> – Louis B. Smedes

God's Expectation to Forgive

Anger and resentment clouds our judgment and leads to exhaustion, disease, and a host of other negative results. Life is too short to live spiritually separated from God on Earth and in Heaven. Yet, so few of us have anything but a vague idea of God's expectation for us to forgive and fewer still have experienced the benefits of forgiveness. They do not understand that failing to forgive means God will not forgive them (Luke 6:37).

> As Michael A. Verdicchio said, "So many times, those who have hurt you have moved on; they no longer even think about it. Yet, there you are, being held captive by your own thoughts and emotions. That is not freedom. Release your anger, bitterness and hurt. Remember, you are not saying that what they did was right. And thirdly, remember that the Bible says that we are to forgive others even as we ourselves have been forgiven."

No doubt one of Satan's desires is to keep us mad at each other. Destructive and negative emotions always crowd out and destroy the best in life. Living with resentment, hate, and planning to get even with those who hurt us brings life to a standstill. Romans 12:19 says, [19] Beloved, never avenge yourselves, but leave it to the wrath of God, for it is written, "Vengeance is mine, I will repay, says the Lord." The need to forgive is exacting and mandated by God. This is the profound truth and simplicity of God's expectation for us.

But God loves us, and he knows what is best for us, even if it's painful at the time.

– Billy Graham

> [25] And whenever you stand praying, if you have anything against anyone, forgive him, that your Father in heaven may also forgive you your trespasses. [26] But if you do not forgive, neither will your Father in heaven forgive your trespasses (Mark 11:25-26 NKJV).

Understandably, while it seems impossible to forgive the sins of others, as a Christian, this is what we must do. Several points to remember are:

- Understand that you have been hurt;
- You do not condone what has happened;
- What was done is wrong;
- Forgive them anyway;
- Do not seek revenge; and
- Keep on forgiving them through daily prayer and reading of the Bible.

Power to Change

To live with hope is to experience a personal relationship with God through His Son, Jesus Christ. Hope enables new ideas and possibilities of a better and more just life. We can thank God for the power to take control of the way we live, what we think, and what we want to become. God knows us best. He knows our strengths and weaknesses. He gives up the power to change from a miserable way of living to one of a forgiving life with the promise of making all things new. It is this gift of love from God that is the greatest blessing to humankind.

- In Jeremiah 31:34, God forgets our sins and remembers them no more.
- In Isaiah 38:17, God puts our sins behind his back.
- In Micah 7:19, God buries our sins in the depths of the sea.
- In Psalm 103:12, God removes our sins as far as the east is from the west.

When we forgive those who trespass against us, we forget their sins. This means that what they did and the turmoil and torment that resulted are buried and blotted out. There is then the freedom to restore relationships with friends and to keep our spiritual walk with God. It comes from our relationship with God and not from the person(s) who sinned against us. As Debra Lohrere said, "Forgiveness releases us from bondage of resentment and bitterness and gives us freedom and peace."

There is power in praying, which is simply talking to God who knows our thoughts and feelings. God is not concerned with how we are dressed, how much money we have, or the words we use in our prayers. What is important is our spiritual growth and attitude. Why not pray the following prayer?

> Dear Heavenly Father,
> Thank you for the forgiveness of my sins and giving me eternal life. Thank you for the courage and desire to forgive those who have trespassed against me. Empower me Lord so that I can embrace the anger and pain. Help me to face my fears and heal the hurt within. Thank you for helping me discern my purpose in life that I was created to do. For Yours is the Kingdom, the Power, and the Glory forever.
> Amen.

Our Greatest Need

An unknown sage wrote, "If our greatest need had been information, God would have sent us an educator; If our greatest need had been technology, God would have sent us a scientist; If our greatest need had been money, God would have sent us an economist; If our greatest need had been pleasure, God would have sent us an entertainer; But our greatest need was forgiveness, so God sent us a Savior."

Jesus Christ is our Savior to whom we pray to abandon resentment, negative feelings, and indifference toward the person(s) who we feel unjustly hurt us and/or hurt a family member. It could be a wife, husband, son, daughter, neighbor, or someone at work. Maybe, the profound feelings of betrayal, injustice, and loss of years of hard work on the job are the result of a combination of several friends who have by their behavior radically changed your personal and professional life and that of your family. Be strong. Learning to think differently is possible with God.

> Dear Heavenly Father,
> Forgive me for holding onto my anger, bitterness, and thoughts of revenge towards those who have wronged me. Please do not allow my heart to be influenced by wrong or evil desires. Help me to think positive thoughts and actions. Help me to take control of my life so that I may experience the freedom and victory of a forgiving spirit. I thank You for forgiving my sins through Your Son's death on the cross for me. Thank You for filling me with the Holy Spirit.
> In Jesus' Name,
> Amen.

Ghandi said, "The weak can never forgive. Forgiveness is the attribute of the strong." So, where does strength come from? It comes from prayer, faith, hope, and love of something better than hate and resentment. It comes from understanding that we can only receive God's forgiveness as we learn to forgive the person(s) who hurt us. The following steps are at the heart of forgiveness through daily prayer:

- Tell your story by writing down the names of people you feel took part in your betrayal, unfair treatment, or something more abusive.
- Visualize the circumstances from which it all took place. Recall the painful parts, especially the minimizing of your

work, beliefs, hopes, and dreams by those who suppressed the truth or outright lied to get what they wanted.

- Try and grasp the "why" of the perpetrator. What were the reasons for the betrayal? Who was behind the injustice?
- Acknowledge that your feelings of bitterness or worse thoughts and/or actions have no place in a Christian's life.
- Thank God in prayer for His Son, Jesus Christ who died for our sins and, therefore, our responsibility to forgive those who sin against us.
- Pray daily to release the offenders from any obligation to make things right, especially since forgiveness should now be understood as a necessity.
- Keep on praying, believing in Jesus Christ, and forgiving the perpetrators as the Lord forgave us.
- Let it go! Regardless of the pain, hurt, humiliation, and lost opportunities, let them go.
- Look forward to a new vision, new feelings, and the ability to wish them well.
- Anticipate the day when you will say to the wrongdoers, "Let us be friends again."

The implication is rather easily understood. If we are not willing to forgive those who trespass against us, God will not forgive us of our trespasses. In addition, God may not be willing to hear our prayers. Not forgiving those who have sinned against us means that they are actually still hurting us and will do so forever. In Matthew 18:21-22 NIV says, when[21] Peter asked Jesus, "Lord, how many times shall I forgive my brother or sister who sins against me? Up to seven times?" [22] Jesus answered, "I tell you, not seven times, but seventy-seven times."

It is important to pray The Lord's Prayer and emphasize with several moments of contemplation the next petition, "Lead us not into temptation, but deliver us from evil." This way, through prayer and surrender to God, He will help us in fighting our personal battles.

Chapter 8

Lead Us Not into Temptation but Deliver Us from Evil

> Let no one say when he is tempted, "I am being tempted by God," for God cannot be tempted with evil, and he himself tempts no one. But each person is tempted when he is lured and enticed by his own desire. Then desire when it has conceived gives birth to sin, and sin when it is fully grown brings forth death.
>
> – James 1:13-15 ES

THIS PETITION IN The Lord's Prayer is frequently misunderstood. God is not going to tempt us to sin? He is not going to set us up to sin against our will. As Dr. Myles Munroe says, "It means that we are to ask God for wisdom so we will not put ourselves into situations that will cause us to compromise our relationship with Him." Having said that, what is also important to remember is that we are free to do as we please. We can either avoid engaging in the wrong behavior or we can live a life of sin. God has given us the freedom to choose. We can do the right thing on earth

Put on the whole armour of God, that ye may be able to stand against the wiles of the devil.

– Ephesians 6:11

and ascend to Heaven when we die or we can commit sin after sin and spend the rest of eternity in hell with Satan.

This petition addresses sins that we are likely to commit if we do not overcome temptation. The way to avoid temptation is to stay awake to the conditions of life and pray so that we do not fall into temptation. "To stay awake" is another way to say, "remain alert" so that we will not be led into temptation that will separate us from our relationship with God. But, of course the reality of every human is that we not only experience many temptations in our lives, we succumb to them as well.

> It is only through this power of Christ within ourselves that we can change.
>
> – Rev. Edward J. Farrell

God or Satan

People of all ages and sex are not tempted by God to seek the desires of the flesh. They have a choice to do something else. It is each person's decision to side with God or with Satan. It is as James 1:2-4 ESV says, "Count it all joy, my brothers, when you meet trials of various kinds, for you know that the testing of your faith produces steadfastness. And let steadfastness have its full effect, that you may be perfect and complete, lacking in nothing." God wants us to be steadfast, perfect, and complete in our love for Him. Thus, it is vital that we regularly turn to God for help, especially when we are faced with persistent temptations.

> Blessed is the man who remains steadfast under trial, for when he has stood the test he will receive the crown of life, which God has promised to those who love him.
>
> – James 1:12 ESV

Throughout life, we are faced with countless good and bad decisions. Once acted upon, the decisions give shape that defines our lives. If we learn to make the right decision to avoid being tempted in the first place, we "may be perfect and complete". On the other hand, lacking the will to do the right thing, the reality of that outcome is not always as we would like it to be. If we are to gain victory over sin, we must pray for help from God to resist Satan.

> By praying The Lord's Prayer, you are asking for God to lead you to a place where you can overcome temptation, just as He promised to do.
>
> – Elmer L. Towns

James 1:14-15 NI says, "...each person is tempted when they are dragged away by their own evil desire and enticed. Then, after desire has conceived, it gives birth to sin; and sin, when it is full-grown, gives birth to death." The truth is we are flawed human beings. Left to our own desires we are lost in sin.

The god of this age has blinded the minds of unbelievers, so that they cannot see the light of the gospel that displays the glory of Christ, who is the image of God.

– 2 Corinthians 4:4 NIV

Thankfully, ***Our Father in Heaven*** is the answer to our fallen nature that craves sin. Every trial in life comes with the potential to do the wrong thing. But, with prayer and the desire to be close to God we can resist the urge to sin. All we need to do is yield to His faithful will. He will help us. God will provide the right escape from the temptation. Also, remember this, you do not need to be a prayer-master to talk to God, regardless of your sins. To talk with God is the key to prayer. God hears us and knows what we need even before we speak (Matthew 6:8).

How do we know this is true? 1 Corinthians 10:13 NIV says, "No temptation has overtaken you that is not common to man. God is faithful, and he will not let you be tempted beyond your ability, but with the temptation he will also provide the way of escape, that you may be able to endure it." So we pray for God to guide us away from temptation and towards holiness. Prayer is the language and the relationship to speak with God. Start by taking a moment to listen to God. You are not alone.

There are two powerful forces in the world: God and Satan. The will of God, our Spiritual Father in Heaven, is that not even one person will perish (Matthew 18:14). The will of Satan is that every human being will perish and end up with him. It is clear that we are tempted by our own lust and also by Satan. If Satan can make a mess of our lives, He will do it. Satan is the evil one. He hates all Christians. His spiritual wickedness is driven by the desire for us to bring dishonor to Jesus Christ and God. He knows that Jesus is the Son of God. Jesus did not fail God when Satan tried to tempt Him in his forty days and forty nights fast in the wilderness. Satan lost the spiritual battle with Jesus. Satan is defeated. He cannot hurt us unless we give him the right to rule over our lives through sin.

Fortunately, for all Christians, God understands the big picture. He created it. With God's help we can grow strong from our weaknesses. We can learn to think good thoughts rather than bad thoughts. With daily prayer, we can be spiritual warriors for Christ rather than victims of Satan's wickedness. After all, Satan is our spiritual enemy. He must be battled with spiritual weapons. 2 Corinthians 10:4 ESV says, "For the weapons of our warfare are not of the flesh, but have divine power to destroy...."

> The awakened consciousness of being, to be in Christ, gives us a capacity to do what we would never dare without Him. There is a power, a strength, a wisdom, a freedom, a Person who really lives in us, activates us, who is our life on the deepest and fullest level.
>
> – Rev. Edward J. Farrell

It is God's Desire

God knows what is in our hearts and minds before we speak the first word in prayer. But, God waits for our feelings, thoughts, ideas, secrets, and concerns in prayer before He will influence us. This journey of our spiritual development takes place as we talk with God in prayer. The good news is that with God by our side He delivers us from evil. Hence, to be open to the grace of God is the ultimate answer to the forces of evil. God is in charge, which is good because He is the only one who has the power to protect us from Satan.

More often than not, life's biggest mistake generally comes when we try to handle everything ourselves. It is God's desire that we find a place for Him in our minds, hearts, and lives. In fact, it is critically important to pray several times daily to connect with God and to sense His presence. We need His support, guidance, and protection if we are to live life as God had planned it from the beginning. This way we can give up our worries and concerns to God for He is in control.

There is no substitute for knowing that we live with God's protection from evil. He loves us and cares for us. Otherwise, we are lost by ourselves. With Jesus, God, and the Holy Spirit, we can come to understand and live spiritual power and discipline. We can live with the certainty that we are loved by our Spiritual Father in Heaven. We can live believing that God will help us make the right decisions in life to avoid the temptations that are all about us day and night.

When we pray to God, He will keep us from falling victim to

our weaknesses that not only will harm us, but also destroy our relationship with the Holy Creator of the Universe. Understandably, all the power and glory belongs to God for helping us to avoid being led into temptation and delivered from the evil one. This means it is important to read the words of Scripture through which we can get close with God, Jesus, and the Holy Spirit. God is real, and He is willing to forgive us of our sins.

> [13] No temptation has overtaken you except what is common to mankind. And God is faithful; he will not let you be tempted beyond what you can bear. But when you are tempted, he will also provide a way out so that you can endure it.
>
> – 1 Corinthians 10:13 NIV

A lifestyle of prayer is the most important task before all of us. Just as a door or any object with mass will not move by itself, our spiritual growth with God is determined by the constant force of our will to pray for a close personal relationship with Him. It is as simple as that. Hence, it is a matter of centering ourselves with God if we are going to live the life God intended for us on earth and in Heaven.

Romans 12:12 NIV says, "Be joyful in hope, patient in affliction, faithful in prayer." John Piper, chancellor of Bethlehem College and Seminary, states what is remarkable about the word "devoted" is that five of the ten New Testament uses apply to prayer.

- **Romans 12:12,** Rejoicing in hope, persevering in tribulation, devoted to prayer.
- **Acts 1:14,** Together they devoted themselves to constant prayer. There were some women in their company, and Mary the mother of Jesus, and His brothers.

- **Acts 2:42,** They devoted themselves to the apostles' instructions and the communal life, to the breaking of bread and to prayer.
- **Acts 6:4,** This will permit us to devote ourselves to prayer and the ministry of the word.
- **Colossians 4:2,** Devote yourselves to prayer, keeping alert in it with an attitude of thanksgiving.

God, Our Father

We pray asking God, Our Father, not to allow us to take the way that leads to sin. We pray to God to keep us from doing the wrong thing. We pray to God to protect us from the evil other people might do to us. We pray to be free from all evil and to be close to God, Our Father in Heaven and the glorious King of the Universe, for He is the God of resurrection and healing.

> "...I am with you always, even to the end of the age" (Matthew 28:20 NKJV).

Chapter 9

For Thine Is the Kingdom, and the Power, and the Glory, Forever

> ...Jesus said, "When you pray, go into your room, close the door and pray to your Father, who is unseen. Then your Father, who sees what is done in secret, will reward you."
>
> – Matthew 6:6 NIV

THE LORD'S PRAYER is finished with the perfect benediction, "***For Thine Is the Kingdom, and the Power, and the Glory, Forever.***" These are words of praise from Jesus about His Father in Heaven. It is the perfect way to end The Lord's Prayer. The wording is very similar to 1 Chronicles 29:11 ESV, "Yours, O LORD, is the greatness and the power and the glory and the victory and the majesty, for all that is in the Heavens and in the Earth is yours. Yours is the kingdom, O LORD, and you are exalted as head above all."

To conclude The Lord's Prayer in this way is to acknowledge that God is in charge. God is of Heaven and not of the Earth. He is our Creator and the Father of our soul. By our faith in Him and His Son, Jesus Christ, we acknowledge a belief that God will rule the Earth as it is in Heaven. He has the "power" to give to us what we need. We thank Him for His guidance in our daily lives by praying ***Thine is the Glory.***

The Kingdom of God is within each person who believes in God. To pray ***Thine Is the Kingdom*** is to acknowledge that God is the Spiritual Kingdom. He reigns upon the Earth and fulfills all His promises and prophecies. He created us, provides for us, and will be with us forever in Heaven. Even our purpose in life is the result of God's power and glory. All that we accomplish in our lifetime is due to God's influence and help for ***Thine Is the Power.***

> **Ephesians 6:10-12,** [10] …my brethren, be strong in the Lord and in the power of His might. [11] Put on the whole armor of God that you may be able to stand against the wiles of the devil. [12] For we do not wrestle against flesh and blood, but against principalities, against powers, against the rulers of the darkness of this age, against spiritual hosts of wickedness in the heavenly places.

Pray According to God's Will

God is our focus in The Lord's Prayer. That is why we pray to Him, and why we think of Him and His Kingdom. We pray that "His Will" be done on Earth. We praise Him in prayer, and we share our thoughts, feelings, and concerns with Him in prayer. We give all the glory to God and His Son, Jesus Christ, for the opportunity to pray The Lord's Prayer.

Prayer according to ***God's Will*** is the key to establishing the right relationship with God. He knows our future and what is best for us. Thus, it is important that our prayers are consistent with His Will and so we must pray with the understanding that His Will is done in our lives. We know that bad things can happen throughout life. We pray to God the Father either to prevent bad things from happening or to change something already bad to something better. Through our faith in God we believe in miracles.

When everything is finally said and done, all of these earthly kingdoms and governments will eventually be taken completely out of the big picture – and the only kingdom that will be left standing for all of eternity will be God's Kingdom, not any of the earthly kingdoms humans have built up down here on this earth.

– Michael Bradley, Bible-knowledge.com

If a prayer is not answered as we hoped it would be, we are comforted by the idea that God believes the alternative is better for us at that particular time and place. As Dorothy Greco says, "Turning our hearts to God in gratitude has the capacity to flip our disappointment upside-down…. The possibility that waiting and suffering have the capacity to transform us offers us profound comfort while crushing our fear of God being fickle. Rather than needing God to answer my accusatory questions of 'Why?' I am free to ask, 'How can I find You in the midst of this?' This inquiry provides us with the traction we need to move beyond our pain and into the transformation that God has for us."

It is our love for God and His positive influence on what we do and how we do it that His love for us keeps us from harm, loneliness, and evil. Even when we are the initiators of our own personal problems, God is with us. This was clear in Isaiah 41:10 NIV, "So do not fear, for I am with you; do not be dismayed for I am your God. I will strengthen you and help you; I will uphold you with my righteous right hand."

Hence, as difficult as it is in dealing with life's challenges, we gain strength in praying to God who said, "Do not be afraid for I am with you." God in Heaven "…He will keep the feet of his saints, and the wicked shall be silent in darkness…" (1 Sam 2:9 NKJV).

Faith in God then, is having the kind of trust and confidence in God and in Christ that leads you to commit your whole soul to Him as Saviour (Justifier, Cleanser, Healer, Deliverer) and Lord (Master, King).

– Michael Fackerell

Yes, the truth is there are wicked people walking about us and living among us. They are interested in stealing, lying, and doing whatever bad deed necessary to get what they want. If they can steal your car, home, or career, they will do so. Often, the victims live in fear and severe mental pain not knowing what to do or how to recover from the sins carried out against them. It can lead to broken marriages, unhappiness, sickness, and disease. More often than not, the anti-depressants, alcohol, and poor mental state result in diseases and disabilities.

Broken promises and loss of trust along with the evil display of words and emotions from others result in such deep pain that millions of people suffer without any help except, perhaps, the idea of getting even. While such thinking may be the human response, it is dangerous for all the obvious reasons. The "getting even" mentality is always wrong. It is always better to depend on ***Our Father in Heaven*** to help us live with the evil acts of others. God is our hope, refuge, and protection in dealing with evil. He is our divine help to get a grip on our sin and that of others that impacts us.

> No temptation has overtaken you but such as is common to man; and God is faithful, who will not allow you to be tempted beyond what you are able, but with the temptation will provide the way of escape also, that you may be able to endure it.
>
> – 1 Corinthians 10:13 NASB

Yes, God is our divine help. But, how many times have we had a conversation with a family member or a friend who was a victim of a senseless act by a colleague(s)? Do you recall him/her saying, "I won't forget. It is just a matter of time before I get even." What the person does not understand is that the negative feelings, if not, hate for the person(s) drains energy from the mind and body. Moreover, it causes that person to forget about other feelings, and sometimes provokes destructive thoughts and actions. Under no circumstances should a person allow him- or herself to get stuck in anger or the idea of getting even.

As difficult as it is, we must forgive those who have sinned against us. We must also use both our intelligence and our faith to work through the anger, hurt, and disappointment. It may take months or years before thinking about who did what without having negative feelings. Life isn't easy, and there is Satan and his helpers that create major roadblocks in marriage, work, and relationships. Here, it is critical to consciously acknowledge what took place and one's true feelings of being injured and feeling intense rage. Understandably, feeling sadness and experiencing waves of grief and anger will pop up from time to time. However, we can choose to pray and ask for God's help in forgiving those who hurt us.

If you are going through some tough times, remember that God will right all wrongs. All the evil and earthly kingdoms will be replaced by God's Kingdom. God's power and glory will reign forever and ever, and we will live without the trials and tribulations of this life. Thus, we need to pray daily that we are blessed with God's constant and unchanging existence, that our needs are met, that we are forgiven of our sins, and that our desires and purpose in life will be conformed to His Will and Glory in bringing God's Kingdom to Earth.

Chapter 10

Amen

The Hebrew word "Amen" affirms our faith in God, through His Son, that His will be done.

THE WORD "AMEN" is used to end a prayer because of its meaning. To say "Amen" is to express agreement with the prayer. It is also taken to mean "so be it" in accordance to the will of God. Jesus Christ said "Amen" many times. He gave us an outline for prayer in The Lord's Prayer (Matthew 6:7-13), in which He concluded with the word "Amen". Thus, when Christians say "Amen", they are affirming their beliefs that what was prayed will take place. "Please let it be as we prayed" is the purpose behind saying "Amen". Stated differently, but with the same meaning, when we say "Amen" at the end of our prayers, we are saying, "Please, Heavenly Father, let that be so."

When we say, "Amen" we are saying, "Yes before God I agree with that; I believe that to be true; I want that to be so".

– Ron Graham

When we talk about our concerns in prayer to God, we are praising Him and honoring His Kingdom when we say "Amen". The Scriptures show this is the case. For example, 1 Chronicles 16:36 says, "Blessed be the Lord, the God of Israel, from everlasting to everlasting. And let all the people say, Amen! Praise the Lord!" Psalm

106:48 says, "Blessed be the Lord, the God of Israel, from everlasting to everlasting! And let all the people say, Amen. Praise ye the Lord."

To say "Amen" is biblical. It is not a meaningless word, and it certainly is not a waste of time. It is scriptural to say "Amen" at the end of a prayer. Hence, saying "Amen" is an overt indication that we believe in God, His Kingdom, and His Glory, Forever. We are telling anyone who hears us that we are praising God forever and ever when we say, "Amen". Praising God and saying "Amen" helps to spread the message that God's Word is the foundation of our faith in John 3:16. It is the Christian's way of pledging obedience to God that He is true and trustworthy in fulfilling our prayers in accordance with His Will.

Dr. Roger W. Thomas introduced an interesting approach to saying "Amen" by identifying numerous scriptures from the New Testament and asking if you will say "Amen" to each one!

1. But seek first his kingdom and his righteousness, and all these things will be given to you as well (Matthew 6:33).
2. For whosoever will save his life shall lose it; but whosoever shall lose his life for my sake and the gospel's, the same shall save it. For what shall it profit a man, if he shall gain the whole world, and lose his own soul (Mark 8:35-36)?
3. And I say unto you, Ask, and it shall be given you; seek, and ye shall find; knock, and it shall be opened unto you. For every one that asketh receiveth; and he that seeketh findeth; and to him that knocketh it shall be opened (Luke 11:9-10).
4. Jesus said unto her, I am the resurrection, and the life: he that believeth in me, though he were dead, yet shall he live (John 11:25).
5. And the times of this ignorance God winked at; but now commandeth all men everywhere to repent: Because he hath

appointed a day, in the which he will judge the world in righteousness by that man whom he hath ordained; whereof he hath given assurance unto all men, in that he hath raised him from the dead (Acts 17:30-31).

6. For the preaching of the cross is to them that perish foolishness; but unto us which are saved it is the power of God (1 Corinthians 1:18).
7. I am crucified with Christ: nevertheless I live; yet not I, but Christ liveth in me: and the life which I now live in the flesh I live by the faith of the Son of God, who loved me, and gave himself for me (Galatians 2:20).
8. Forbearing one another, and forgiving one another, if any man have a quarrel against any: even as Christ forgave you, so also do ye (Colossians 3:13).
9. Seeing it is a righteous thing with God to recompense tribulation to them that trouble you; And to you who are troubled rest with us, when the Lord Jesus shall be revealed from heaven with his mighty angels (2 Thessalonians 1:6-7).
10. If any man among you seem to be religious, and bridleth not his tongue, but deceiveth his own heart, this man's religion is vain (James 1:26).
11. If we say that we have no sin, we deceive ourselves, and the truth is not in us. If we confess our sins, he is faithful and just to forgive us our sins, and to cleanse us from all unrighteousness. If we say that we have not sinned, we make him a liar, and his word is not in us (1 John 1:8-10)

The Lord's Prayer begins with Jesus addressing Our Father in Heaven and closes with "Amen". From the beginning to the end of the prayer, the focus of the prayer is on God. The purpose of the prayer is to teach us to pray by affirming God's sovereignty, seeking forgiveness of our sins, and conforming our desires and purpose in life to His Will and glory.

It is important to remember that Jesus cautioned us against "rote repetitions" (Matthew 6:7) and praying to impress others. For example, " But when ye pray, use not vain repetitions, as the heathen do: for they think that they shall be heard for their much speaking. Be not ye therefore like unto them: for your Father knoweth what things ye have need of, before ye ask him" (Matthew 6:7-8). Jesus also said, "...when you pray, go into your room, close the door and pray to your Father, who is unseen. Then your Father, who sees what is done in secret, will reward you" (Matthew 6:5-6 NIV).

Epilogue

> I am glad that I have a Heavenly Father who cares for me. I can go to Him with my most important needs and know that He cares for me and that he can meet them.
>
> – Jimmy Chapman

CHARLES H. SPURGEON said that ***The Lord's Prayer*** is not a prayer intended for the masses, but is instead a prayer for the true disciples (believers) of Jesus Christ, those who have been converted by the saving grace of God. Every word in the prayer is important. "Our" can mean that we do not pray alone. The word "Father" helps us to feel that we are not alone and God cares for us. "In Heaven" means there isn't anything that God can't take care of. He has the power to hear us and to answer our prayers. God is our Spiritual Father and we are his children. All we need to do is "ask" and yet, James 4:2 says, "Ye have not, because ye ask not."

Jesus is the bread of life.

Pastor Kevin Ruffcorn says, "Prayer is one of the most common experiences of humankind – at least in the United States. Almost everyone (98%) says they believe in a divine being, but only half of the people say they worship on a regular basis – and that regularity could be Christmas and Easter. Still, almost two-thirds of Americans say that prayer is a part of their lives." Why is it we are so reluctant and/or so lazy that we do not take the time to pray? The neglect of prayer is not good, especially since there is no other way to connect with God. We must give ourselves daily to prayer. A person or family that prays can decrease fear, worry, and anxiety in accordance with God's Will. Failure to pray closes the door to God.

It is through prayer that God provides for our needs. His grace and power are linked to prayer that promotes holiness and growth in our spirituality and closeness to God. To pray is to be in intimate time and space with God where we can search our thoughts, renew hopes, and give comfort to the fact that we are part of God's everlasting family. The Bible states this many times throughout the scriptures. For example, Psalm 139:23-24 says, "Search me, O God, and know my heart! Try me and know my thoughts! And see if there be any wicked way in me, and lead me in the way everlasting."

> The most tragic thing that has happened is that we have forgotten the God-power within us. This power is the essence of what we are. It gives us strength and determination to live, to pray to God, and to thank His son for all that He did for us on the cross.

When we pray to the Lord, we are spiritually blessed. There is the opportunity to know God's path, truth, and the fullness of prayer. This is stated in Psalm 25:4-5 ESV, "Make me to know your ways, O LORD; teach me your paths. Lead me in your truth and teach me, for you are the God of my salvation; for you I wait all the day long." In other words, the focus of prayer is on God, His ways, discerning His will for our lives, and fulfilling His purpose in our lives.

Most people are professional worriers. If only they would trust fully in God, they would have little reason to be anxious and afraid.

Praying for God's Will to be done on earth and trusting fully in God we are free to live His purpose in our lives without feeling lost and anxious. In Matthew 6

(ESV) just after he teaches The Lord's Prayer, Jesus expands on this when he says, [25]…I tell you, do not be anxious about your life, what you will eat or what you will drink, nor about your body, what you will put on. Is not life more than food, and the body more than clothing? [32]…your heavenly Father knows that you need them all. [33]… seek first the kingdom of God and his righteousness, and all these things will be added to you.

We have a Spiritual Father in Heaven who loves us. He cares about us, and He invites us to connect with him in **The Lord's Prayer**. This is why Jesus came to the Earth. He opened the way to God for us so that we can know **Our Father**. This is why Jesus gave us The Lord's Prayer. So, why not pray the prayer daily? Why not share it with your friends, family, and colleagues?

Jesus, the Son of God, made it possible by his blood that was shed on the cross. Our sins have been paid for by the Son of God, Jesus Christ. Now, it is our task to get to know Our Father who is the Father of creation from which we are the children of the Creator.

> [28] Come to me, all you who are weary and burdened, and I will give you rest. [29] Take my yoke upon you and learn from me, for I am gentle and humble in heart, and you will find rest for your souls. [30] For my yoke is easy and my burden is light.
>
> – Matthew 11:28-30

God does not want us to be anxious for nothing, and He does not want us to worry about tomorrow and what tomorrow may bring. We come to this understanding by praying to God and turning over to Him our worries, fears, and anxieties. To pray The Lord's Prayer is to express trust in ***Our Father in Heaven*** to completely handle our problems. We know this is true, given that Jesus said: "All that you ask for in prayer, believe that you will receive it and it shall be yours."

Pray at home with your family. Teach your children how to pray. Meditate on the Bible and pray to God, "Lord, what do you want me to do?" Remember to listen in silence after praying the prayer of hope, The Lord's Prayer. God is our Father. He was revealed to us by his Son, Jesus Christ, who died on the cross for our sins so that we may have eternal life with Him in Heaven.

The Lord's Prayer can be prayed exactly as is or parts of it can give rise to feelings or thoughts of a given day, night, situation, or a concern in a person's life. The following brief comments of each section of the prayer should help finalize your connectedness to The Lord's Prayer.

Our Father

It may seem strange to refer to God as "Father" much less "Our Father" because we have an earthly father to whom our minds refer to when we say, Father. When the words Our Father are spoken in The Lord's Prayer, a few seconds of reflection on God, Our Father, may help in appreciating our personal relationship with God that this particular prayer makes possible. We are one of His adopted children.

Who Art in Heaven

Imagine, if possible, the essence of "what is" Heaven. Obviously, our minds are not capable of doing justice to God's Heaven. But, nonetheless, why not pause to allow your mind and body to be raised to "somewhere" other than earth. No, the process is not easy, but it does become easier over time. With the heart's desire to know God and our place of eternal existence, we may get a glimpse of God's reality.

Hallowed Be Thy Name

Isaiah 6:3 speaks of a vision in which God surrounded by celestial beings who cried, "Holy, Holy, Holy is the Lord...." Similarly, note the "Holy" implied in the Isaiah 46:9, "...I am God, and there is none else; I am God, and there is none like me." Here, it may be helpful to pause just after saying ***Hallowed Be Thy Name*** and let the truth sink in for you are praying to the one and only God of the Universe. Allow yourself to feel relaxed and confident that He hears you and is participating in your prayer.

Thy Kingdom Come

Of course it is impossible to actually imagine God's Kingdom on Earth, because the idea itself is huge. God's Kingdom will be without diseases, bad weather, wars, and politics. There will be peace and love throughout the Kingdom. God's goodness, purity, and love will move all of us to another level of human kindness. Our future is safe with God in His Kingdom.

Thy Will Be Done, on Earth as It Is in Heaven

God's Will comes full circle, first the Garden of Eden and now on Earth as it is in Heaven. Here, it is imperative that we learn God's Will and then do our best to bring our will into harmony with His Will. This petition requires an honest look at who we are, what we do, and the challenge of completely giving our lives to God. This means confessing our sins to God and keeping the prayer door open to do so constantly in daily prayer.

Give Us This Day Our Daily Bread

The word "Bread" refers to all of the different needs (such as physical, mental, social, and spiritual) that help to bring us closer to the Will of God. Such needs may stem from our prayer life or the lack of it, our work habits, faithfulness, or the need or failure to admit our sin and ask forgiveness. Also, if we should have evil thoughts in our hearts, we must ask God to provide a daily dose of spiritual healing to deliver us from evil.

And Forgive Us Our Debts as We Also Have Forgiven Our Debtors

"Forgive us as we forgive" is a statement of our relationship with God who will forgive us of our sins if we forgive others of their sins against us. In short, we ask forgiveness knowing that we must be willing to forgive as well. This means that the goodness of God must flow through us to others, especially since "For all have sinned, and come short of the glory of God…" (Romans 3:23-24).

And Lead Us Not into Temptation, but Deliver Us from Evil

Temptation itself is not a sin. Everyone is tempted (even Christ), but not everyone remains sinless. However, temptation becomes sin when we yield to it. When we allow our minds to contemplate bad ideas and evil thinking (such as getting back at someone who hurt us), that is bad. We pray to God to deliver us from evil regardless of where it comes from, to give us strength to do the right thing, and the power of God to keep us on the right path.

For Thine Is the Kingdom and the Power and the Glory, Forever

God is the sovereign King. His authority and dominion speaks volumes. God doesn't just possess all the power, He "is the power" that created everything and has power over the Universe and the Earth. He has the omnipotence to execute His power. God's glory belongs to Him. There is nothing we can do to add to it or take from it.

Amen

The Lord's Prayer is concluded affirming that the kingdom, the power, and the glory belong exclusively to God, ***Our Father in Heaven*** forever and forever. Thus, our final response is "let it be" — Amen!

Bibliography

Adinolfi, M. The Lord's Prayer (Matthew 6:9-13). http://www.christusrex.org/www1/pater/excursus.html

Allen, C.L. (1960). ***All Things Are Possible Through Prayer.*** Westwood, NJ: Fleming H. Revell Company.

Allen, C.L. (1965). ***The Ten Commandments: An Interpretation.*** Westwood, NJ: Fleming H. Revell Company.

Amen. (2008). **Encyclopaedia Britannica.** (Online). http://www.britannica.com/EBchecked/topic/19143/amen

Amsterdam, P. (2011). ***The Heart of It All: The Nature and Character of God's Holiness.*** (Online). http://directors.tfionline.com/post/heart-it-all-nature-and-character-holiness/

Bahr, G. J. (1965). Use of the Lord's Prayer in the Primitive Church. ***Journal of Biblical Literature***. 94;2:154.

Baillie, D. M. (1948). ***God Was In Christ***. New York, NY: Charles Scribner's Sons.

Barth, K. (2010). ***The Doctrine of the Word of God.*** Vol. 1, Part 2. Peabody: Hendrickson Publishers.

Batten, J.D. and Hudson, L.C. (1966). **Dare to Live.** West Nyack, NY: Parker Publishing Company, Inc.

Boone, T. (2002). **The Power Within: The Integration of Faith and Purposeful Self-Care in the 21st Century.** Bloomington, IN: AuthorHouse.

Boone, T. (2011). **A Father's Gift of Prayer.** Bloomington, IN: AuthorHouse.

Bounds, E.M. (1978). ***Purpose in Prayer.*** (Online). http://www.goodreads.com/ book/show/2276010.Purpose_in_Prayer

Byargeon, R.W. (1998). Echoes of Wisdom in the Lord's Prayer (Matt 6:9-13). ***Journal of the Evangelical Theological Society.*** 41;3:362.

Dunningham, L.S. and Kelsay, J. (2002). ***The Sacred Quest: An Invitation to the Study of Religion***. Upper Saddle River, NJ: Pearson Education, Inc.

Davies, P. (1992). ***The Mind of God: The Scientific Basis For A Rational World.*** New York, NY: Simon & Schuster.

Duquoc, C. and Greffre, C. (1972). **The Prayer Life.** New York, NY: Herder and Herder.

Evely, L. (1965). ***Teach Us How To Pray.*** New York, NY: Newman Press.

Farrell, E.J. (1972). ***Prayer Is A Hunger.*** Denville, NJ: Dimension Books.

Fagal, W.A. (1965). ***By Faith I Live.*** Nashville, TN: Southern Publishing Association.

Fox, E. (1938). ***The Lord's Prayer.*** (ebook). Harper-Collins Publishers. http://www.absolute1.net/emmet-fox-the-lords-prayer.html

Fullam, E.L. (with Bob Slosser). (1980). ***Living The Lord's Prayer.*** New York, NY: Ballantine Books.

Ghandi, M. (2000). ***The Collected Works of Mahatma Gandhi.*** (2nd Edition, Volume 51, pp. 301-302. Mahatma Ghandi Young India, New Deli: Government of India, Publications Division.

Glynn, P. (1977). ***God: The Evidence.*** Rocklin, CA: Prima Publishing.

Gorsuch, J.P. (1990). ***An Invitation to the Spiritual Journey.*** New York, NY: Paulist Press.

Greco, D. (2013). ***When God Doesn't Answer Prayer...At Least How We Want Him to Answer It.*** http://www.relevantmagazine.com/god/practical-faith/when-god-doesn%E2%80%99t-answer-prayer

Gredinger, R.K. (2012). ***The Power of Forgiveness.*** Huffpost Healthy Living. (Online). http://www.huffingtonpost.com

Grou, J.N. (1965). ***How To Pray.*** Springfield, IL: Templegate.

Gula, R.M. (1999). ***The Good Life: Where Morality & Spirituality Converge.*** Mahwah, NJ: Paulist Press.

Hamlin, R. (2014). ***The Truth About the Lord's Prayer.*** https://www.guideposts.org/blogs/on-the-journey/the-truth-about-the-lords-prayer

Hanson, B. (2002). ***The Lord's Prayer: An Eight Part Series Exploring its Meaning Line by Line.*** http://www.explorefaith.org/prayer/essays/lord5.html

Haring, B. (1978). ***Free and Faithful in Christ: Moral Theology for Clergy and Laity*** (Volume 1: General Moral Theology). New York, NY: The Seabury Press.

Haughee, C. ***The Lord's Prayer.*** http://lifehopeandtruth.com/god/prayer-fasting-and-meditation/how-to-pray/the-lords-prayer/

Hicks, J.M. ***The Theology of The Lord's Prayer.*** http://dsntl8idqsx2o.cloudfront.net/wp-content/uploads/sites/10/2008/05/lords-prayer.doc

Hinn, B. (1990). ***Good Morning, Holy Spirit.*** Nashville, TN: Thomas Nelson Publishers.

Holy Bible, New International Version. (2011). Biblica, Inc.® Used by permission. All rights reserved worldwide.

Hong, E. (1984). ***Forgiveness Is A Work As Well As A Grace.*** Minneapolis, MN: Augsburg Publishing House.

John 3:16. ***King James Bible "Authorized Version."*** Cambridge Edition. http://www.kingjamesbibleonline.org/John-3-16/

Jones, T. (2005). ***The Art of Prayer.*** Colorado Springs, Colorado: WaterBrook Press.

Kilmon, J. ***The Lord's Prayer.*** http://www.historian.net/lp-pap2.html

Lawrence, B. (2004). ***The Practice Of The Presence Of God.*** Uhrichsville, Ohio: Barbour Publishing, Inc.

Leech, K. (1980). ***True Prayer: An Invitation to Christian Spirituality.*** New York, NY: Harper & Row, Publishers.

Lewis, G.R. and Demarest, B.A. (1996). ***Integrative Theology.*** Grand Rapids: Zondervan, Bk. 1. p. 233.

Lohrere, D. (2006). ***The Power of Forgiveness.*** (Online). http://scripturetruth.blogspot.com

MacDonald, B. (2015). The Lord's Prayer. ***Discipleship Training Institute / Lion Tracks Ministries.*** http://www.NotJustAnotherBook.com/thelordsprayer.html

Milne, B. (2009). ***Know the Truth, A Handbook of Christian Belief.*** Downers Grove: InterVarsity Press.

Munroe, M. (2002). ***Understanding The Purpose and Power of Prayer.*** New Kensington, PA: Whitaker House.

Odhner, H.Lj. (1972). The Lord's Prayer. http://newchristianbiblestudy.org/bundles/ncbsw/on-deck/english/books/Lords%20Prayer%20-%20Odhner.html

Omartian, S. (2006). ***A Book of Prayer.*** Eugene, Oregon: Harvest House Publishers.

Orloff, J. (2011). ***The Power of Forgiveness: Why Revenge Doesn't Work.*** (Online) *Psychology Today.* Sussex Publishers, LLD.

Osterhage, S. (1996). The Lord's Prayer: An Esoteric Interpretation. ***Sunrise Magazine.*** Theosophical University Press. http://www.theosophy-nw.org/theosnw/world/christ/xt-oste.htm

Packer, J.I. ***Attributes of God, Part 2.*** Lecture 11, Transcendence and Character.

Pawson, D. (2007). ***Is John 3:16 the Gospel?*** ISBN 978-1-901949-55-1

Pitre, B. (2006). The Lord's Prayer and the New Exodus. ***Letter & Spirit.*** 2:69-96.

Quiery, W. H. (1967). ***Facing God.*** New York, NY: Sheed and Ward.

Rahner, K. and Metz, J.B. (1981). ***The Courage to Pray.*** New York, NY: Crossroad.

Ripley, F.J. (1951). ***This Is The Faith.*** Billings, England: Birchley Hall Press.

Rolheiser, R. (1999). The Holy Longing: The Search for a Christian Spirituality. New York, NY: Doubleday, a division of Random House, Inc.

Seligman, M.E.P. (1994). ***What You Can Change and What You Can't.*** New York, NY: Knopf.

Simpson, S. (2000). ***The Lord's Prayer, Our Prayer.*** http://www.deceptioninthechurch.com/lordsprayer.html

Sloyan, G.S. (1962). ***Christ The Lord.*** Garden City, NY: Echo Books, a division of Doubleday & Company, Inc.

Sponheim, P.R. (1988). ***A Primer on Prayer.*** Philadelphia, PA: Fortress Press.

Strauss, E. (2014). ***Good Always Wins.*** Uhrichsville, OH: Value Books.

Tada, J.E. (1991). ***Seeking God: My Journey of Prayer and Praise.*** Brentwood, TN: Wolgemuth & Hyatt, Publishers, Inc.

Tan, P. (2007). ***The Spiritual World.*** Peter Tan Evangelism, Canberra: Australia.

Thomas, R. (2001). ***Let All God's People Say AMEN.*** SermonCenter. (Online). http://www.sermoncentral.com/sermons/let-all-gods-people-say-amen-roger-thomas-sermon-on-lords-prayer-69214.asp?Page=1

Thomas, R. (2001). ***Honoring God's Name.*** SermonCenter. (Online). http://www. sermoncentral.com/sermons/honoring-gods-name-roger-thomas-sermon-on-lords-prayer-69148.asp

Thurston, B. (2009). ***For God Alone: A Primer on Prayer.*** Notre Dame, ID: University of Notre Dame Press.

Torrey, R.A. (1924). ***The Power of Prayer.*** Grand Rapids, Michigan: Zondervan Publishing House.

Towns, E.L. (1997). ***Praying The Lord's Prayer For Spiritual Breakthrough.*** Venture, CA: Regal Books.

Veninga, R.L. (1985). A Gift of Hope: How We Survive Our Tragedies. Boston, MA: Little, Brown and Company.

Watson, T. (1687). ***Man's Chief End Is to Glorify God.*** Fire and Ice Sermon Series. (Online). http://www.puritansermons.com / http://www.puritansermons.com/ willard/will0001.pdf

Wellman, J. (2014). ***The Lord's Prayer – Meaning and Lessons From The Our Father Prayer.*** http://www.patheos.com/biogs/christiancrier/2014/05/13/the-lords-prayer-meaning-and-lessons-from-the-our-father-prayer/

White, M.S. (2013). ***I AM the Bread of Life. Series: God's Self-Revelation.*** (Online). http://mmpcalbany.org/sermons-i-am-the-bread-of-life

Witvliet, C.V., Ludwig, T.E. and Vander Laan, K.L. (2001). Granting Forgiveness or Harboring Grudges: Implications for Emotion, Physiology, and Health. ***Psychological Science.*** 12:117-123.

Wright, N.T. (2001). The Lord's Prayer as a Paradigm of Christian Prayer. In: ***Into God's Presence: Prayer in the New Testament***. (Ed., R. L. Longenecker). Grand Rapids, Eerdmans, 132-154.

Yancey, P. (2006). ***Prayer: Does It Make Any Difference?*** Grand Rapids, Michigan: Zondervan Publishing House.

Printed in the United States
By Bookmasters

RELIGION - SPIRITUALITY

One critically important step in dealing with life's dilemmas and unpleasant experiences is to trust in Jesus Christ as the Son of God and say "yes" to prayer. This means trusting in God to help live in the present. It means pushing aside doubts and relying on The Lord's Prayer to affirm the good in life for Jesus said, "These things I have spoken unto you, that in me ye might have peace. In the world ye shall have tribulation: but be of good cheer; I have overcome the world" (John 16:33). Life is not hopeless.

Late in the evening while completing a boat ride on the Taylors Bayou in Southeast Texas, Ed and I decided to write a book about The Lord's Prayer. After almost a year we compared our notes and the effects of reading and analyzing the prayer. We were shocked to find how comforting it was to say The Lord's Prayer. We examined the prayer line by line and ultimately felt the need to share what we had learned. Neither of us can imagine living day-to-day without the spiritual comfort of being with "Our Father In Heaven" and knowing that God forgives us of our sins as we forgive those who have sinned against us. Thank you Jesus, the Son of God for dying on the cross for our sins and for sharing The Lord's Prayer with the disciples.

U.S. $11.95